Affirmations for Adult Children of Abusive Parents

Also by Steven Farmer:

▼

Affirmations for Adult Children of Abusive Parents

▼▼▼

Steven Farmer
with Juliette Anthony

Lowell House
Los Angeles
Contemporary Books
Chicago

Library of Congress Cataloging-in-Publication Data

Farmer, Steven.
    Affirmations for adult children of abusive parents / Steven Farmer
with Juliette Anthony.
        p. cm.
            ISBN 0-929923-60-X
        1. Adult child abuse victims—Rehabilitation.   2. Affirmations.
I. Anthony, Juliette.   II. Title.
RC569.5.C55F38   1992
616.85'822—dc20   91-34063
                                                              CIP

Requests for such permissions should be addressed to:
Lowell House
2029 Century Park East, Suite 3290
Los Angeles, CA 90067

Publisher: Jack Artenstein
Vice-President/Editor-in-Chief: Janice Gallagher
Director of Marketing: Elizabeth Duell Wood
Design: Gary Hespenheide

Manufactured in the United States of America
10 9 8 7 6 5 4 3 2 1

CONTENTS

▼▼▼

For Diane

▼

HOW TO USE THESE
AFFIRMATIONS

▼▼▼

Because of your experiences with abuse, you learned a lot very early about yourself and your world. Whether you drew these conclusions yourself or were told them by adults in authority, they became beliefs entrenched in your subconscious.

The purpose of using affirmations is to develop new ways of thinking about yourself and your world, new beliefs that are more generative and life-giving than the destructive or limiting ones you've held up to now. By working with the affirmations in this book in the prescribed ways, you will not be simply "brainwashing" yourself. Instead, you will be working with a process of releasing your old, habitual ways of thinking and feeling, and you will find that you can actually influence your feelings by what you are telling yourself.

When you first use this book, I suggest that you choose one of the 26 topics and work initially with three affirmations within that topic. Later, as you become more familiar with the techniques of using affirmations and with your own responses, you can move around the book, choosing the ones that fit your particular needs.

The 3 x 3 Method

The method that seems to work the best is called the "3 x 3." For the first three weeks, focus on three affirmations. At the end of three weeks, pick three new affirmations and work with those for the next three weeks. Continue this pattern until you reach the twelfth week. At that time, assess how effective each affirmation has been. How much has your thinking changed? Have you been able to change the way you interact with people in this area of concentration? Choose those affirmations you wish to continue working with and add new ones, always working in groups of three. Don't overload yourself; back off any time you feel you are pushing too hard.

Repeat each affirmation *slowly* 10 to 15 times at a sitting or until your initial reaction shifts. Do this twice each day. Work with each specific affirmation for at least 21 consecutive days to achieve the full benefits.

Alternative Ways to Affirm

Here are five other techniques to help you use the affirmations effectively:

1. You can simply say the affirmation out loud using your first name, for example, "I, Steven, enjoy the continuing stability I've created in my life." Using your first name emphasizes your personal participation and commitment in the process. Do this when you are alone. Your car is an especially good place because saying affirmations uses your driving time in a positive way.

Listen closely to your thoughts and feelings and note how your body feels. Does your body tense up or feel weak? Just notice the reaction without dwelling on it. Once you have observed the reaction, return to the affirmation and repeat it, once again noticing your reaction. Continue until you have finished the desired repetitions.

2. Divide a piece of paper down the middle with a pencil. Write the affirmation in the left-hand column and your reaction in the right. Your reactions may surprise you. Continue until you have finished the desired repetitions.

3. You can also say the affirmation using pronouns with your name, for example, "I, Steven," "You, Steven," "He(She), Steven." Say the affirmations out loud or write them out. Once again, go through all the instructed repetitions.

4. Try using a tape recorder to record the affirmations, saying each one only once with a short pause in between, or repeating them a few times. When you play back the tape, repeat each affirmation as you listen to it. This is useful later when you are working with a number of affirmations at the same time.

5. With a partner, state the affirmation and have your partner state it back in the second person to affirm you. You say, "I, Steven . . ." and your partner says in return, "Yes, you, Steven . . ."

Some Guidelines

As I suggested in my earlier book, *Adult Children of Abusive Parents,* work with a journal every day. As you work with these affirmations, record in your journal any of the thoughts or feelings that are happening as a result of specific affirmations. You might write, "Today I forgot about being afraid to speak out in class, and my professor was very complimentary about my presentation. That's a first."

As you work with these methods, you will undoubtedly arouse a lot of feelings because you are challenging a familiar system of thinking about yourself that you have held for years. You will challenge these traditional patterns of thought by introducing and repeating new thoughts to yourself. A myriad of emotions will be provoked, including anger, hurt, sadness, rage, relief, and joy. If you get such a reaction, don't be concerned. The affirmation is reaching its intended target. If the reaction is too strong or if there is little or no reaction, then you can either modify the affirmation, making it more or less intense, or you can skip that affirmation altogether and move on to another one. A moderately strong reaction is actually desirable.

Some of the affirmations contain specific instructions in the text following the affirmations. These are only suggestions for using that particular affirmation in a specific way.

▲

You can refer to this section of the introduction for help in using any of these affirmations.

The most important aspect of using these affirmations is that you find what is most comfortable and works most effectively for you.

I would like to acknowledge the support and contributions of the following people: Reverend Sioux Harlan Elledge, August Priest, Marilyn Sharon, Dr. Toni Bradley, Michael Lindsay, and Alan Garner. Thank you all for your generosity and wisdom.

Steven Farmer
Laguna Beach, California
September 1991

ACCEPTANCE

▼▼▼

Because you suffered physical and emotional indignities as a small child at the hands of obviously misguided and sometimes even evil adults, acceptance may seem especially hard. The most helpful method of acceptance, the Serenity Prayer, hangs on the walls of the 12-Step programs: "God, grant me the serenity to accept the things I cannot change; courage to change the things I can; and wisdom to know the difference."

You cannot change your past or the experiences you lived through, but you can transform the pain you suffered into power for the present moment in your life today. You can reach out and get help to work through your pain and accept what happened. Also, you can learn new skills for living a good life today. This is not a simple process if you were literally devastated by the abuse in your childhood. But acceptance means dealing with what we can today. The following affirmations will guide and support you in this process.

I accept the reality of my life, with all the seemingly good and bad.

▼▼▼

Putting this affirmation into practice in your life may require a good deal of emphasis on your spiritual program. You need to look to your Higher Power to lift you over the hurdles of hurt and frustration you are carrying from your childhood abuse. There is a wonderful book by Rabbi Harold S. Kushner, *When Bad Things Happen to Good People,* which some Adult Children have found very helpful.

Brenda raged at her mother for a year after her mother died. She felt she was treated badly in the will, just as she had been all of her life, even though she was left with a financial cushion that most would consider a real blessing. Brenda's unwillingness to simply accept these conditions deprived her of the happiness and freedom she might otherwise have enjoyed, and ultimately she became physically ill. Fortunately, the illness awakened acceptance in her. While Brenda was recuperating, she had plenty of time to think. She realized she was ruining what could be an enjoyable present by refusing to let go of the lifelong abuse she had suffered from her mother. Once she realized she was far better off simply accepting reality, she saw her illness as a blessing that would direct her into a new life.

Accepting the reality of today allows you to make the most of what you have whether it appears to be good or bad, however much it differs from what you thought you ought to have. Make the most of what you could have, or what was owed to you that didn't happen. If you can accept that, you will have triumphed over one of life's biggest problems; letting go of the past pain that we know and can control in our minds, to live in the unpredictable reality of today.

Living in today is real acceptance.

I accept the greater good in all my friends and acquaintances.

▼▼▼

When you have unreasonably high expectations of your friends and acquaintances and do not gracefully accept the errors they make, you put constraints on the relationships that are as unrealistic as your original expectations. Looking at the bigger picture, accepting the greater good in people, and accepting their imperfections without trying to fix them, makes your relationships more comfortable and mutually beneficial.

However difficult it is to forgive and forget the betrayals of your childhood, don't make your current friends the victims of your past doubts and criticisms. Keep your mind open and know that every mistake today does not bring about the kind of disaster that happened with mistakes made when you were a child.

Honestly accepting your friends makes your life much warmer.

I am relaxed with who I am.

▼▼▼

What a wonderful feeling to be relaxed at long last, to accept yourself as you are. When all you knew was criticism from your parents, it is very likely that you internalized a lot of that criticism, discouraging yourself at every turn from being the competent and caring person that you truly are. The way to overcome this discouragement is to start again, this time with the knowledge and confidence that you can dismiss any negative voices inside your head because you know they are just your parents' voices recorded for posterity in your subconscious. Now you can change posterity!

When you say this affirmation, breathe deeply and relax all the way inside your heart, where your self-acceptance will grow more firmly into a permanent part of you.

I accept joy, humor, and laughter
in my life.

▼▼▼

There isn't much joy in abusive households, and the laughter is frequently limited to ridicule. Expanding your emotional capacity to accept joy, humor, and laughter may be a tall order, but it is a worthwhile and possible one. Now that you are aware that there are so many other Adult Children very much like you, some of the burden of thinking you were the only one is lifted. And when you start listening to other people's stories, you may find it absurdly funny that many people seem to share the same mothers and fathers.

Lifting the burden of being alone opens up your life. There is room for laughter now. Watching the comedies on TV is appealing and enjoyable, and spending an evening at the local comedy club is a lot of fun now, whereas before you used to be unable to let go and laugh. You can now relax a little bit. You are on your way to truly better times.

Going out with your friends or just sitting outdoors and watching the clouds roll by makes sense when the feeling of impending doom has left your life. You will find there is so much open space in your life now. When you accept joy, humor, and laughter into that space, there is a wonderful healing.

I accept my physical being as it is right now.

▼▼▼

Picking on your physical being is one way to avoid taking positive action to maintain your looks and your health. Choosing to accept yourself and feel loving toward yourself can free the energy to move your body in any direction you want.

Bruce finally stopped complaining about being overweight and started walking every morning with a friend for an hour. After a few weeks, people were telling him how wonderful he looked. He started to feel so good about himself that the cinnamon rolls and apple pie didn't seem nearly as inviting, and gradually he lost 25 pounds that he had been carrying around for two years ever since he stopped smoking.

Bruce accepted where he really was and took one action on which he felt capable of following through. The good results and the momentum created by that action triggered changes that ultimately allowed him to lose weight. You have to start where you are to do something on your own behalf.

Combating self-criticism by accepting yourself and then taking positive, beneficial action can give you the ability to make choices in your life that you wouldn't have ever thought possible.

I accept fulfillment in every area of my life.

▼▼▼

When you focus positive energy on your goals, they are much more likely to be fulfilled than if you say, "Oh, that will never happen to me." Richard kept believing that his desire for fulfilling work in his field of architecture would indeed happen. He used the affirmation "I accept fulfillment in the area of my work" and pursued the necessary footwork. He brought his résumé up to date, delivered it in person to people who could directly help him, and mailed it to a carefully chosen list. One of his friends got a job in a well-known architectural firm and told Richard to apply also as the company was "staffing up." Richard not only got the job, he has excelled and been given raises over the past three years.

Accepting that fulfillment is available to you, doing the work to pursue it, and then accepting it joyfully when it happens in your life are the paths to a far richer life. Staying open to positive, fulfilling experiences is a life-supporting way to spend each day.

When you replace your negative expectations with a positive affirmation, "I accept fulfillment in every area of my life," you give yourself the best chance to make your expectations become reality.

I accept the peace that has come to me through doing the work of recovery.

▼▼▼

The peace of acceptance comes after breaking through the denial and experiencing the anger and the sadness. Although you can't stay in denial forever and the old feelings surface again and again—but with less intensity—your overall approach to life gradually becomes one of acceptance and peace. You could describe it as finally knowing what's what, and letting it go at that.

Sometimes life can be brought down to a few simple common denominators, but perhaps for you it just isn't that simple. It seems to take a long time to let go. Rest assured that there are still oases of peace as you make your journey, places where you really do feel peaceful for short periods of time before you get caught up in your life or are thrown back once more into the grief and sadness.

Treasure these pockets of peace and know that they are harbingers of a much more peaceful life to come when you have worked through a bigger portion of your pain. Accept them as rewards for doing as much as you have done and enjoy the time that you do have, tasting what peace is like for you for the first time in your life.

Peace can be a natural part of living.

BALANCE

▼▼▼

Congratulate yourself on entering uncharted territory: the area of balance. Metaphorically speaking, your parents probably lived at ultimate extremes, either at the North Pole or the South Pole. Moderate climates in between did not exist for them. Since you never actually saw balance in your family, it is something that you can learn by observing the behavior of people you feel are balanced and by being aware of your tendencies to think of things in extremes—all bad or all good, all happy or all miserable—and moderating them. Your life will be much calmer without the extremes. The following affirmations will support you in your efforts to be balanced.

I now have a balanced
and fulfilling life.

▼▼▼

With your journey into recovery well under way, you can begin to envision this affirmation coming true for you. To have a balanced and fulfilling life requires willingness to make choices on your own behalf on a daily basis. These choices allow you to maintain your equilibrium. Sometimes you may choose to limit the activities in a day, to turn down a tempting invitation to go out, because you recognize that you need rest if you are going to be balanced tomorrow. Sometimes it means that you choose to keep calm in the face of an upsetting situation, recognizing that being hysterical doesn't help you or anyone else. You are choosing balance and the health that comes with it over the out-of-control emotional responses from your childhood.

By concentrating on this affirmation, you can begin to feel the presence of real calm in your body and mind. Everything starts to become more fulfilling because you are able to participate in everything you do.

I maintain my balance in the
face of difficulties.

▼▼▼

Reading a book of affirmations and agreeing with what it says is one thing; remembering to put these affirmations into action in your life is another. By using this affirmation on maintaining your balance several times a day, you will keep in your consciousness the idea that you have choices as to how you act and feel. When you are faced with difficult situations, you can choose to stay calm and in a balanced frame of mind. You can actively choose growth by deciding to react calmly rather than blindly, which you might have done in the past.

You can incorporate this affirmation into your life slowly with practice. Balance is a goal that reaps rewards even when it is achieved little by little. Just a bit more balance than you had before might make all the difference in the outcome of a difficult situation.

I keep a balanced perspective as I make changes in my life.

▼▼▼

One thing that could happen while you are making so many changes in your life is that you become as over-involved in the process of making changes as you were during the abuse. Some of you may feel that because you waited so long to deal with your issues, you want to move as fast as you can now that things are finally happening. The old adage "Hurry up and slow down" applies well here. Remember that you are primarily in the process of living, and that getting over the effects of childhood abuse has its place in that process.

Keeping your energy distributed in a balanced way among your work, social activities, exercise, rest, and recovery is the purpose of this affirmation. When you find yourself spending too much time on one area of your life, take some time out. Repeat this affirmation, and refocus on maintaining a balanced perspective on all areas of your life.

**I remember to inventory my actions
throughout the day and take corrective
measures to keep balanced.**

▼▼▼

Keeping your balance while changing your life patterns requires monitoring during the day to make sure you are on track. Just take a few minutes to do a spot check. "Am I hungry, lonely, angry, or tired?" is one-spot check inventory suggested in 12-Step programs. If you tend to skip meals and several hours later find yourself off balance as a result, monitor yourself every few hours. Making sure that you take the time to eat can improve your ability to deal with stressful situations when they come up during the day. When you are hungry or overtired, you can overreact. Feeling guilty and rectifying things that get out of control demands a lot of energy.

Taking the time to check your body and your feelings is preventive maintenance. You don't ever have to get that far out of balance. Your life will have many fewer ups and downs. A spot-check inventory, such as the one suggested in this affirmation, can be a great energy saver, a real gift to yourself.

I enjoy the rewards of balance
in my life.

▼▼▼

Taking your life off the roller coaster, choosing balance over chaos, brings the reward of serenity, something you might not have thought possible after years of unpredictable behavior with abusive parents. If you have continued the usual pattern of abuse in your own life, taking up where your parents left off because it was the only kind of life you had known, it may take some time to adjust to the calm atmosphere you can now create for yourself. You are giving yourself a chance to rest and to achieve better health, even though you may feel the loss of all the excitement you usually create. Enjoying a different kind of life by taking long nature walks, spending quiet evenings at the movies, and taking time to organize your personal life certainly lacks the adrenaline rushes of the old drama-and-rescue routines but wears much better in the long run. If you find compatible people in Adult Children of Alcoholics (ACA), Co-Dependents Anonymous (CoDA), or other 12-Step programs who are also trying to break the old patterns, planning new healthy activities together makes it much easier.

The rewards of balance are all around you every day. Learning to appreciate them is a big part of staying balanced.

I keep my balance in daily life between work and play, responsibility and pleasure, love for others and solitude.

▼▼▼

Leading the kind of life where you divide your time among healthy activities could be completely new to you. If you have been the superresponsible workaholic, for example, now is the time to consciously learn to play and to cut back your concentration on work. There are adult classes of all kinds offered at your local YMCA or YWCA; including bridge, tennis, ballroom dancing, folk dancing, carpentry, and painting. In the extension division of your local community college, you might find weekend camping trips, fiction or poetry writing workshops, or drama and music classes. If you have spent much of your time running from responsibility and "enjoying" yourself, but you're no longer happy, try taking some classes to support your work skills or help you advance.

Devoting all your time to being with other people may not have left you time to take care of your own business. You can reassess how much time you need for yourself and balance that with time for your family and friends.

It has probably felt natural and easy to go all out in some areas and neglect the others. Making the change to a balanced life may feel awkward at first, but you will find it rewarding and enriching as the months go by.

I am moderate in all my activities, and my body stays balanced.

▼▼▼

The desire to go overboard, to be as perfect as possible in all the things that you undertake, is common for Adult Children from any kind of dysfunctional family. Losing yourself in anything and everything has been one way of escaping the shame surrounding your abuse. Now you have a chance to moderate everything in your daily life. You can soften and slow down your voice. If you hurry wherever you go, give yourself a little extra time and walk more slowly, quieting your emotions at the same time. If you tend to eat on the run, try sitting down and talking with someone else while you are taking the time to enjoy your meal. Also, see if you can keep the number of activities you get involved with at a manageable level.

Moderation means commitment to yourself first. The resulting quiet that you achieve allows balance in your body. Your body responds in a much healthier way when you pace yourself and respect your limitations.

I enjoy the continuing stability I've created in my life.

▼▼▼

S tability" used to be an unfamiliar word for you because being stable felt like being lifeless. Unless there was big excitement in your life, constant upheaval and drama, you really did not feel that you were alive. Your nervous system had become accustomed over a lifetime to being constantly on edge. One of the benefits of recovery is the quieting down of outside stimuli and the transition into enjoying day-to-day living.

Anna came from an army family that had moved nearly every six months. She never knew a stable home, long-term childhood friends, or an uninterrupted education. As an adult, Anna had moved thirteen times in three years. Within a few weeks of living in an apartment, she would find something that she just couldn't stand. One time it was the neighbors fighting in the next apartment; another time it was the garbage truck that came at 6 A.M.; still another time it was the street light that shone too brightly into her window.

When Anna recognized the pattern in therapy and realized that she could not have a stable life unless she learned to stay in one place for a reasonable amount of time, she surrendered her desire to move incessantly and began working on developing closer relationships with her new friends in recovery. She started fixing up her apartment with the intention of staying there for some time to come. Today she enjoys plants, a pet bird, and cooking dinner for someone she asks over, all new activities in her life.

Stability is nurturing. It helps you toward better mental and physical health. Say this affirmation often to accelerate your healthy progress.

BOUNDARIES

▼▼▼

Boundaries let you *and* other people know who you are. You can't really appreciate all that you are until you feel a sense of being contained within boundaries. Without boundaries, you are like a leaf in the wind, at the whim of whoever wants to use your energy to meet his or her needs. Many Adult Children who have been abused have no boundaries and continue to give themselves away in codependent ways. What if for the first time you were conscious of your own energy and used it to meet your own goals?

By using the following affirmations to set boundaries, you can become free, free to interact in new ways, no longer destined to repeat the past. By taking small steps each day and setting limits in your present circumstances, you can help to heal the hurts of your childhood. Old wounds will not constantly be triggered by new violations. Setting boundaries, saying yes to your own needs, lifts you out of the past and into a new way of life.

I can say yes to my own needs even if they conflict with those of others.

▼▼▼

Having boundaries in your personal or business relationships is critical to your health and the health of the relationships. Boundaries tell you where the other person ends and where you begin. When you stop sacrificing yourself in order to take care of and stop seeking approval from the other person, you can get in touch for the first time with what you really like, want, and need.

Joanna decided to stop meeting her mother's needs every time they went out to lunch. Instead of letting her mother choose where they went, as she usually did, Joanna said she would like to go to a small Italian restaurant where they had never been, because she loved Italian food and wanted to do something for herself. Her mother fussed at first, but Joanna remained firm, saying that this was her choice, something she wanted to do for herself.

Having your boundaries clearly stated saves you a great deal of time. You state where you are and what you want instead of leaving it up to others to define your needs and wants for you. They often miss the mark, leaving you feeling resentful and used. With boundaries, you have choices.

**I set limits with my friends regarding
the time I am available to them in
person and on the phone.**

▼▼▼

Setting new boundaries in old friendships can often meet with resistance. Some of your friends may like the "old" you, who would drop whatever you were doing at a moment's notice to pal around with them, or who was the most wonderful and only friend they knew whom they could call to pick them up from the airport at midnight. They may not believe your new self-caring stance in life. You are no longer operating at their convenience, and this makes them uncomfortable. It's a big change. You may need support from a good friend, sponsor, or therapist who can help you through this transition. You are risking a lot. Some of your old friends may not be willing to go through the changes necessary to keep the friendship and may part ways with you. As a result, you may start to experience the fear of abandonment from your childhood.

Stop! Give your catastrophic thinking a course of correction. It is helpful to remember that only infants, not adults, can be abandoned. And there are millions of people in the world, any number of whom might be better for you at this stage of your life than the person who is leaving.

If you continue to care for yourself, you will not only survive, you will thrive—and feel better than you have ever felt.

**I set limits on unacceptable behavior
from my family and friends.**

▼▼▼

Now that you are developing boundaries, you may discover that what you thought was your good-natured generosity of spirit was in fact caretaking and people-pleasing. You may have even taken pride in your ability to be tolerant and compassionate in the face of outrageous behavior. This belief has allowed the abuse so familiar from your childhood to continue to harm you in the present.

Breaking patterns with those closest to you is difficult. These people have a heavy investment in keeping us the way we were. If we change, they cannot continue to get their needs satisfied in the old way. Setting straightforward limits—"If you are drinking, you may not come to my home," or "You may no longer criticize the way I live while you are in my home"—will be difficult at first and may be met with resistance from your family and friends. But *you* will feel better about yourself, and will begin developing a much stronger sense of self.

I feel safe in any situation when my boundaries are strong.

▼▼▼

Strong boundaries give you the knowledge that you can take care of yourself no matter where you are. You are vulnerable only when *you* make the choice to be open and close to another person. This is a new concept, for in the past you have been at the receiving end of behavior from people who have not respected your boundaries.

Developing that safe feeling is a gradual process. On some days, you will set two or three boundaries that are small steps on the path to safety. Soon you will begin to feel safe when you make a major boundary shift in an area where you haven't been taking care of yourself. You can say to yourself, "No more overtime at work without being paid," and the quality of your life will change instantly.

I respect the boundaries of others.

▼▼▼

If no one respected your boundaries, you could not learn to respect the boundaries of others. As a child, you may have borrowed things without asking because you were afraid that the answer to your request would be an irrational no. Or you may have minded other people's business just to get a handle on what might happen to you. Those behaviors helped you to survive as a child, but now they make it more difficult to get along with other adults, both in personal and business relationships. Respecting other people's boundaries helps keep each person comfortable by considering his or her wishes and privacy.

If you need advice about respecting the boundaries of others, ask your sponsor or a friend with good recovery for guidance.

Ask someone you know who is excellent at respecting the boundaries of others to help you put this into practice. Your interactions will immediately become easier.

I define my boundaries specifically.

▼▼▼

"This week, I will be unavailable in the evenings," you might say to a friend, setting a definite period of time. "But I need you to give me a lift to two meetings," replies your friend. While repeating the above affirmation silently to yourself, keep saying out loud your boundary statement, "This week, I will be unavailable in the evenings." You do not have to explain yourself or acknowledge the other person's feelings unless you want to. Explaining is an old habit that gives the other person a chance to change your mind. And unless you want to run that risk, it is wiser not to open things up for discussion.

Boundaries are a reflection of what you believe. Setting specific boundaries clarifies your feelings about everything in your life.

I can tell someone pleasantly when I don't want to be touched.

▼▼▼

Many of us who were sexually or physically abused have understandably confused boundaries regarding touch. When someone touches you, it's difficult for you to trust that it doesn't mean ultimate physical or sexual harm. Marjorie was unaware that she shuddered involuntarily every time someone tried to put an arm around her until one of her boyfriends commented, "Someone must have hurt you really badly. You always jump when I put my arm around you."

It takes work to uncover those patterns and start integrating into your relationships normal responses to touch. While you are going through this process, it is certainly all right to say without feeling defensive, "No, thank you. I'd rather not be touched just now." Stating your preference or simply saying, "No, thank you. I need some space today," is well within your rights.

Your physical boundaries are your absolute rights.

I am creating boundaries for myself where I had none before.

▼▼▼

It is often a real shock to discover the concept of boundaries and to become aware simultaneously that in many areas of your life you have had absolutely none. Instead, you have been participating in the familiar dysfunctional "spaghetti syndrome," in which you become completely intertwined with other people, your work, and your recreational activities. You can't tell where you end and they begin.

Frank realized that when he walked into a group of people, he immediately tried to "merge" with someone or some piece of furniture in the room. If you feel this overwhelming need to merge to overcome the feeling of being separate, there is basic boundary work that you can start doing right now.

Instead of accepting this "urge to merge," start looking at what is going on inside you each time it happens. At first you may feel uncomfortable, and you may experience symptoms of withdrawal because you have used merging as a survival mechanism for so long. Work through this, and you will start to become aware of boundaries and begin to emerge as your own person.

There is an immediate difference in your everyday life when you create boundaries.

CHANGING YOUR THINKING

▼▼▼

You can dramatically increase your control over your feelings by working on your thinking. You may think that the events in your life—your car breaks down, you don't get the job you wanted, your friend doesn't return your phone call—determine how you feel.

If you look deeper, however, you will see that it is your *beliefs* about what has happened, not the events themselves, that make you feel the way you do. Shakespeare wrote, "Nothing is bad or good but thinking makes it so." If you experience extreme anger, hurt, or depression, you are probably suffering from irrational thinking. You may be catastrophizing, making unreasonable demands, or taking personally things that have nothing to do with you. You engage in these methods of dealing with situations or feelings naturally because you witnessed them in your childhood home.

These affirmations can help you become aware of how certain irrational beliefs may cause difficulties in your life, and what you can do to change these beliefs so that your life will be much easier each day.

I let go of catastrophizing and gain rational perspective on every situation.

▼▼▼

When you have spent a lifetime being abused in dangerous situations and the only way you know how to get your adrenaline pumping is to create "dangerous" situations for yourself, catastrophizing can become a devastating habit. It can actually create the events that you fear. If you think your mate or spouse is going to leave you each time you make a mistake, even though he or she has given you no indication that that would happen, the likelihood is that you are catastrophizing.

If you carry your fears into acting as if he or she were going to leave, you will create a peculiar nonreality in your relationship. You are reacting completely irrationally to something that doesn't exist, and your spouse or mate has no way of making you feel more comfortable since he or she had nothing to do with it to begin with.

You are the only one who can do something about this. Write in your journal, "What is the worst that could happen?" and imagine the most outlandish outcome. Could you survive it? The answer is probably yes. Now ask yourself *realistically* what is the worst that could happen. You will see that even if the feared event does occur, it will not be nearly as disastrous as what you had fantasized.

Remember that nothing is ever as important as we think.

I modify my unreasonable demands on life by using more rational self-talk.

▼▼▼

If you consistently demand that life and other people, especially you, live up to your own very tough rules, you probably talk to yourself and others using shoulds, musts, and have tos. You are following rules and regulations your parents passed on to you, or you have become so accustomed to their style of thinking that you are good at making up rules yourself. When you approach life in this rigid manner, you can stay isolated and lonely without being aware that you are causing your own difficulties.

When you soften the way you talk to yourself, you may very well find that you lessen the unrealistic demands you make that have been leaving you unhappy for many years. When you look at what you want in life and write it all down in your journal, you will see a realistic picture form of what is motivating you in everything you do. For example, you may find that underneath your resentment toward your mate is your unreasonable demand that you shouldn't have to work. You have demanded for yourself a life-style that doesn't exist for you at the current moment and makes you needlessly unhappy with the life-style you have.

Try to use this affirmation and talk with yourself more reasonably. Make a list of your unreasonable demands, all your "should" statements, in your journal and see if they don't seem out of line when you read them on paper. Try substituting the word "prefer" for "should" in all the demands and see if they sound different now. Using preferences, you can deal more rationally with the way things really are.

When we change our demands into preferences, life suddenly becomes much easier.

I am now free of needing anyone's approval, and I am the best judge of my own actions.

▼▼▼

Letting go of your old beliefs about yourself is a gradual process in the journey of recovery. Some beliefs that come from our abusive childhoods are truly crippling. Joan believed that she had to have everyone's love and approval or she felt, literally, as if she would die. This was a belief that Joan had carried with her ever since childhood and had never examined for its validity today, and it was making it impossible for her to enjoy life. Affirmations are extremely effective in changing this sort of belief, which has its roots in a life that no longer exists. When Joan examined how she developed this belief and faced her feelings about the many times she had been abandoned as a child, she was able to separate her past life from her present life for the first time.

By using this affirmation, you are freeing yourself from old beliefs and gaining trust in who you are today.

I can do everything now according to my ability, without the yardstick of perfection.

▼▼▼

When you see only perfection, you are bound to be unhappy all the time, and in your mind nothing will ever measure up to your standards. You will probably run the idea of failure through your mind before attempting a project and convince yourself that you might as well not even make the effort. Sooner or later you will have to accept that you and life are imperfect at best.

You can help yourself reduce perfection to the level of acceptance by making an effort to do something in a mediocre way—*consciously*. If you are used to having an immaculate house, try doing something that would normally bother you. Don't make the bed today, or leave your dishes in the sink for several hours. See if these things really affect your life in the drastic way you thought they would. You may discover that your not being perfect isn't quite as disastrous as you thought it was going to be, and you will let go little by little of your rigid standards.

When you relax your perfectionist standards, you begin to like yourself for all the things you can do that you thought you weren't good enough at before. With just a change in your thinking, you suddenly have a broad base for self-esteem.

I now accept life on life's terms.

▼▼▼

When you endure the grave injustices of emotional, physical, or sexual abuse as a child, you wait for the day when you can escape from your house and everything will be different. You believe that life will be fair once you have left the abuse and should go according to your plan. After all, you have suffered enough, and now the world should make up for all the hurt of your childhood. Unfortunately, life is simply what it is. Other people will get jobs that you felt were meant for you, and you might not get the raise that you are sure you deserve. If you continue to get angry over these kinds of things, it's time to consider changing your thinking.

To make progress in life, you must deal with things as they are, not as you wish they were. Having unrealistic expectations only causes pain. If you find yourself repeatedly disappointed, see if you don't feel less agitated and more comfortable by giving up your expectations in favor of preferences. For those items that are strong preferences, ask yourself what you can actually do about them. Create a plan of action and follow through with it.

You can have a preference about something in life and take action on it without being upset.

Today I honor what I remember about my childhood.

▼▼▼

In your teens, you may have had startling memories of abuse that happened when you were five or six years old. You questioned your parents and were told that it was just your imagination.

Today, when memories burst through the tight fabric of denial that you wove to protect yourself from your own knowledge, you can honor the thoughts and memories that come to you. They are messages from a part of you that needs to heal, and you have permission to honor those messages. It helps to talk with other family members who were present during the serious abuse because they frequently remember—sometimes better than you do—many of the details.

Memories can come back slowly, especially if you have had no memory at all of certain years during your childhood. Learn to listen to yourself, to hints of what happened to you so that you can finally heal.

You have the right to all that you remember. It is there to help you heal.

I am now motivated by enthusiasm in everything I do.

▼▼▼

Not so long ago, you might have been motivated by a fear of failure or the need to gain someone else's approval. You could never give yourself credit for the good work you were doing. Nothing you did was good enough. You compared yourself to other people and always came up short.

Changing your thinking about yourself does take time. Building self-esteem is a process that takes commitment, but if you take overly high standards out of the equation, it immediately becomes much easier to feel comfortable undertaking a task. If you stop yourself every time you criticize your own performance or compare yourself to someone else, your stamina will increase miraculously. Change your thinking to reassure yourself that you are doing very well and that what you are doing has only to do with you, not with anyone else's performance.

You may notice a change in how you feel as a result of changing your thinking. You are actually removing a block that prevented you from enjoying anything that you tried to do. With the self-criticism gone, you can enjoy and become enthusiastic about whatever you do.

It is up to each of us whether to live our lives with enthusiasm or fear.

I give myself credit now for all the wonderful things that I do.

▼▼▼

Perhaps you come from a family where your parents took all the credit for anything the children accomplished. Your father said to you, "You inherited all your ability from me, and if it weren't for my connections, you would never have amounted to anything. This statement robbed you of being a person. You learned to credit other people for all your talents. Your parents kept their powerful positions by claiming everything you did was because of them, leaving you without the benefit of knowing who you are.

Today, if you win recognition at work or school, value those accomplishments for yourself and change your thinking about them. Get used to feeling that these accomplishments belong to you and that you don't owe them to your family or anyone else. You might practice saying "Thank you. I appreciate the recognition. I worked very hard for it," so that when the day comes, you will be comfortable and able to claim your honor for yourself.

It takes only a small change in your thinking to make a big difference in your life.

COMMITMENT

▼▼▼

We have the opportunity for commitment in every aspect of our lives, in our relationships, in our work, with our friends, and most of all with ourselves. While you can go through your whole life putting commitments to others and to outside affairs before commitments to yourself, you will ultimately experience "burnout" because you will not be nurturing yourself physically and emotionally.

Ironically, the physical or emotional illness caused by burnout can put you on the sidelines for long periods of time, which in turn can break those seemingly top-priority commitments to others. And sometimes you simply feel compelled to drop the ball and take off, which also breaks those commitments. Not honoring a commitment to yourself means that you are likely not to keep your commitments to others either.

Because you grew up in an abusive family, you may have witnessed many broken commitments, including divorce, which broke your parents' original commitment to each other and to their children. In some cases, divorce can damage your ability to trust other people or circumstances and can set a precedent for you to start breaking commitments in your own life.

Today, commitments are a part of our adult lives. If we don't pay our bills, our electricity or phones are turned off. Yet many of us resent these intrusions into our lives until we make a real commitment to ourselves. Then the burdens of everyday life seem far less worrisome.

The following affirmations encourage you to look at the commitments in your life and evaluate your level of participation in each commitment.

I am committed to working a program of recovery.

▼▼▼

Before you are able to change very much in your life, you will have to commit to working some sort of program of recovery. Unfortunately, recovery does not work by casually dropping in at a meeting or a therapist's office every now and then, or picking up the phone and calling someone once a month. It is difficult to stay on the path to recovery, but it becomes much easier when you have made a commitment.

You are probably wondering what is involved in making this commitment, and you might be thinking that you don't like yourself well enough yet to make any kind of commitment to yourself. It is best that you make the commitment to yourself anyway, acting "as if" you already care about yourself, because that commitment to yourself and your beliefs will carry you through the darkest hours, when you feel like giving up and acting out your particular self-destructive behavior. Only you can deal with yourself inside your head and your heart.

It pays to make a commitment to yourself to stick to a program of recovery because you and your program are your best defense against those moments when you might choose behavior that could destroy you.

**I maintain contact with my friends
through good times and bad times.**

▼▼▼

When you make a commitment to stay in touch with your friends, it means that you are there for them in happy times, when they are celebrating, and in difficult times, when they are ill or hospitalized. One of the side effects of an abusive childhood is difficulty in being consistent with people. Another side effect is a tendency to isolate yourself when things get too rough, to stop reaching out or allowing others to reach in.

Monica never had real friends until she got into recovery. She had been severely abused by her father, physically and emotionally, but since her mother and brother never acknowledged the abuse, she didn't dare mention her vague memories to anyone. She hid from herself and tried to hide from others.

When she found a therapy group, she heard stories similar to hers, in which the abuse had also been totally unacknowledged. Monica began to make friends. Her self-designed imprisonment was over, and she was sharing in the group, but her habit of years of social isolation were harder for her to break. By making a commitment to call two women each day and finding them willing to listen to her, Monica began to change the way she related to other people.

When Monica required surgery and was hospitalized for nearly a week, she was happily surprised when she received bouquets of flowers in her room and visitors from her group each afternoon. She had made commitments to her friends, and they in turn made commitments to her.

Commitment to others can bring wonderful, unexpected rewards.

I am committed to achieving my goals.

▼▼▼

Setting goals and making commitments to attain them are two different things. There are many people who are off and running with a new project every six months. They can always come up with ideas that they immediately turn into objectives without doing the careful planning needed. When their hard work does not pay off six months later, they simply find another project. Somehow, they manage to get by financially.

When you are committed to achieving your goals, you are willing to do the planning and consulting with others that is required to come up with a realistic goal. Philip wanted to branch off from the medical secretarial service where he had worked for five years. He knew the boss was charging clients three times what he was paying Philip. Philip's goal was to make a living working for himself. He talked it over with several doctors he knew personally, and they gave him solid encouragement.

After quitting his job, Philip distributed flyers and got four new clients. He now makes at least three times what he was making at his previous job. Planning realistically and being committed to follow through are of major importance in achieving your goals. Being in the right place at the right time and being fortunate are helpful, of course, but they often come about when you have done the necessary footwork to know where you want to go.

Commitment is essential to achieving your goals.

I am committed to treating myself well.

▼▼▼

When you decide to make yourself top priority for the first time in your life, it will take some time to make changes. Putting yourself first is *so* different from the way that you have lived all of your life that you will have to make a major commitment to be successful. This commitment involves choosing healthy food for yourself and the way you choose to look when you leave the house each day. It means that you think about the consequences to your health before you undertake something physically dangerous or taxing and the consequences to your time and energy of favors that you do for others without a second thought.

Initially, if you take time for regular exercise and insist on your own activities for fun, you can make a gradual adjustment with your family and friends, building up to bigger and better commitments as you and they become accustomed to your new way of handling your life.

Making a commitment to treat yourself well may be difficult, but you will feel so much better about yourself by keeping that commitment.

I am committed to clarity and honesty in all my dealings.

▼▼▼

In most abusive families, children don't have the chance to witness honest, clear exchanges between their parents. The lack of clarity, working in tandem with denial, creates an atmosphere in which honesty doesn't exist.

Clear and truthful transactions with other people are essential for genuine friendships and intimacy. You may know someone like Michael, who is extremely charming and seems to know everyone, but who no one else seems to really know very well. Interchanges with him are pleasant, but after you speak with him, you are quite unclear about what transpired in the conversation. He is unable to be honest about himself. He cannot be a friend.

Honesty is the conduit for development of ourselves and intimacy with others. If you are honest with yourself, you have a chance to overcome whatever handicaps you have, and you have the opportunity to become a genuine person who other people will come to know and love. Honesty and clarity in dealing with others can bring you respect and a chance to live in peace.

Honesty is the best policy for a reason—it works!

I am committed to being of service in my community.

▼▼▼

To recover from the abuse you suffered as a child, it is helpful to be part of a community that is meaningful to you. Overcoming the isolation that abuse causes is useful in developing the skills you need for the remainder of your life. The group can be any kind of community organization—a church, a school, a nonprofit service organization, a therapy group or 12-Step program—where there will be an opportunity for you to volunteer your personal energy for the benefit of others. Many times, keeping your service commitments can be the one thread that keeps you going in this tough time of early recovery. You have people who expect you to be somewhere at a specified time and a contribution you are counted on to make.

Whether you have avoided commitments altogether or taken on too many at once, now is the time to practice balance in your life with one or two meaningful service commitments, such as singing in the church choir, working for a nonprofit organization, serving meals at a homeless shelter, or volunteering for a job at one of your group meetings.

When you do service for others without expecting anything in return, it improves your spirits and sense of belonging.

I am committed to being the best
that I can be.

▼▼▼

Self-pity is a tough enemy to conquer, especially when you have perfectly good reasons for it. You were abused. Your parents took opportunities away and gave you no support for your individual efforts to be your own person. But self-pity doesn't take away any of what has already happened. It only takes away your ability to do positive things for yourself in the present.

Whatever has happened in your childhood may have sidetracked you considerably and slowed you down in many ways. Now it comes down to what you will do for yourself today. Whatever time you have lost cannot be regained, but if you invest in yourself right now, whether it is changing jobs, going back to school, or developing your creative talents, you will be doing for yourself what you wish your parents had done for you. Now you have to be your own parent and provide all these opportunities for yourself.

You can do for yourself today whatever it is you need to become the best possible you.

COMPLIMENTING YOURSELF

▼▼▼

Compliments of any kind were probably rare in your house when you were a child. If you came home from school in the afternoon, excited about the A you got in science, and you tried to speak well of yourself to your family, you may have been told, "What about your piano lessons? You're not doing so well at *them*." Your parents often took away any good feelings you might have had about yourself. Maybe they were uncomfortable around good feelings, or maybe they thought that if you felt good inside, they would lose control over you. Eventually, you didn't bother to sing your own praises. In fact, all the criticism from your parents became a resounding committee inside your head, stalking and shadowing you every time you made an effort on your own behalf. Now you can stop the committee and tell it to be quiet—or in even plainer language, to shut up! You can talk back out loud every time it says something negative.

You can begin to practice complimenting yourself by working with the following affirmations. While it will take time to overcome all the old negativity, the good feelings you will develop are ultimately well worth it.

I appreciate the wonderful person
that I am.

▼▼▼

When you say this affirmation, the committee in your mind could start up again with those criticisms from your childhood: "Who do you think you are?" or "What makes you think you're so wonderful?" It may be hard for you to strengthen the voice inside you that is repeating the affirmation, telling yourself that you are wonderful in the face of so much opposition. You must be persistent.

If you do an honest review of all your qualities, using a close friend as a sounding board, you will begin to get a more realistic picture of who you are, with all your wonderful attributes alongside of what you've been told about yourself all your life. It's pretty hard to operate effectively in the world when every step you take is blocked by a wall of negativity. If you are persistent in staying with this affirmation, you can climb over that wall and overcome that negativity.

Complimenting yourself every day, telling yourself that you are, indeed, a wonderful person, is a jumping-off place for you to begin to change the thoughts that influence the choices you make in your life.

If you are feeling good about yourself, your choices will be positive and life supporting.

I am a competent and caring person.

▼▼▼

Many Adult Children from abusive families have no true picture of how accomplished they are or how truly caring they may be. Maybe you are one of those competent and caring people who got no appreciation from your parents. Everything you did was questioned or diminished. As a child, you may have felt that your reality was constantly being taken away and that you were helpless to do anything about it. Now you have a chance to claim your own reality.

Using positive self-talk and complimenting yourself every day through these affirmations can make a significant difference in the confidence you have about your abilities and feelings.

I am very competent at my job.

▼▼▼

Maybe you are not employed right now in the kind of work you really want to do, but if you put forth your best efforts and do competent work, your feelings about yourself will improve and your options for the future will open up. You are probably already doing very fine quality work but are not acknowledging your own efforts.

If your work could use improvement, tell yourself that you are very competent at your job every day. This will help you lift your performance level, and you will feel appreciated even if no one else notices. When you genuinely feel good about the work you do, you will make much better choices about how to conduct yourself on the job. You will react to situations from a centered and solid place inside yourself, and your judgment and actions will reflect that. Both you and your employer will benefit.

Reminding yourself that you *are* competent brings benefits in attitudes as well as actions.

**I make valuable contributions to my
own life and to other people's lives.**

▼▼▼

Thinking in terms of contributing to your *own* life and well-being in addition to contributing to the lives of others may be a first step for you, but using this affirmation to achieve new balance in your life is wonderful progress toward valuing what you have to offer yourself and the world. When you come from an abusive family, placing yourself second after everyone else was survival and was expected. Now, in realizing how much you have to offer yourself and balancing that with what you can do for others, you come to see the possibilities of a much richer and healthier life.

Contributing to others means contributing to yourself.

I am an interesting person and very good company.

▼▼▼

Focusing on things that interest you and participating in activities that you are enthusiastic about enable you to share yourself with others in ways that can be fun for you and your friends. By using this affirmation and feeling positive about yourself, you can begin to explore new activities. You can learn golf or t'ai chi or sing in a choir no matter what your age, or enroll in extension classes at your local community college where you can meet other people who are also looking to expand their lives. Your good feelings about yourself help you to be receptive toward things coming into your life. A willingness to join others in activities, and the good friendship skill of actively listening to what new acquaintances tell you about themselves, can make you very good company.

You can continue to become an interesting person, and others will enjoy your company.

I am an intelligent and capable person.

▼▼▼

If you came from a family where you were constantly asked, "Why are you so stupid?," every time you make a mistake today you hear those same words echoing in your mind. You can counteract this. Tell yourself over and over that you are an intelligent and capable person no matter what happens and no matter what you hear the committee in your head telling you. Try writing down all the negative thoughts that come up about yourself in your journal and trace them back to exactly who said those words to you. Mark a big X across the page and "talk back" to the person who said the words. If your grandfather told you that you were lazy, and those words echo in your mind whenever you have a job to do, you might say, "Grandpa, I don't appreciate it when you talk to me that way. I will not permit you to call me lazy ever again." You are becoming powerful on your own behalf.

Always complete your exercise with the positive affirmation that you are a wonderful person.

I have learned to forgive others and myself so that my life is full of love.

▼▼▼

When you come from an abusive household, to learn how to forgive is an important task. It is a major accomplishment and worth complimenting yourself when you have recovered to the point where you are able to forgive your abusive parents, forgive yourself for being abused, and operate in the world today with forgiveness in your repertoire of emotional behavior. The love you can offer to others is accompanied by kindness and compassion.

Jim finally expanded his capacity for love when he was able to forgive his father for beating him repeatedly for what seemed like trivial offenses—leaving the top off the peanut butter jar or not rinsing his dishes when he put them in the sink. Jim learned only recently that his two younger sisters experienced the same kind of abuse, but the three children were afraid to talk about it when they lived at home for fear of being caught and punished further. Each child suffered in isolation, thinking he or she was the only one, until they were all on their own and started comparing notes.

Once Jim learned that he was not singled out for being the worst child, that his father was equally abusive to all the children, he felt a huge burden was lifted off him and was able to forgive his father for being a tormented man. The bitterness that he had carried around for years lifted slowly but noticeably, and he was much more caring toward his two younger sisters than he had been in his whole life. People were attracted to him now and wanted to be friends with him because he was loving and kind.

It is indeed worth complimenting yourself when you have made forgiveness a part of your life and can watch love replace all the loneliness and bitterness that you used to feel.

COURAGE

▼▼▼

To have courage means that you keep going in the face of fear and tremendous odds. It took enormous courage to endure the abuse of your childhood and to continue to care and have hope. If you survived that pain by becoming a substance abuser, it took courage to get clean and sober. If you are codependent, it took great courage to face the dependencies you have had with your abusive parents and the dependencies you have repeated with others, and to gradually let go and begin your own life for the first time. Setting out on your own path, where everything you do feels new and different, is the most courageous journey of all.

But look around. There are other people also on that path. You can offer one another comfort and share these affirmations together.

I have the courage to accept my life as it is one day at a time, and to set goals to improve it.

▼▼▼

It takes courage to truly face the reality of the life you have had one day at a time, because you survived your childhood by learning how to escape what was happening to you. Facing reality takes practice. It is so much easier to live in fantasy, to say, "Someday, I will do differently" and avoid the challenge of choosing what you can do today.

Only with the acceptance of today will any of us begin to make changes that improve the quality of our lives. On the gameboard of life, you must begin at the square where you actually are. That takes a great deal of courage for anyone who has been abused. With the philosophy in this affirmation, you can start a new direction in your life, one that is firmly based in reality.

It takes more courage to accept than it does to fight.

I have the courage to be honest with myself.

▼▼▼

After years of denial, being honest with yourself takes immense courage, especially being honest with yourself about what things were really like in your childhood. Some things you just didn't remember until now because the pain was too great. Before you started recovering, you were probably very critical of yourself. If you had started remembering then, you would have taken responsibility for everything and punished yourself for things that no child could have caused. As you learn who you really are by examining yourself and your life without self-justification *or* self-loathing, with the compassionate detachment you might show toward someone else, you will free much of your spirit and strength which has been used to keep all of this stuff from the past hidden.

Share what you have discovered with a person you trust. You will feel wonderfully unburdened.

I now face all situations in my life with courage.

▼▼▼

Facing new situations with courage can change the way you live each day. At first, it may be that you act "as if" you had courage, that you watch how others you admire handle themselves in their everyday lives and imitate their behavior. When you were growing up, you had no role models for handling your life with courage. Abusive parents are not usually courageous. You now have permission to choose role models for the new way you wish to live. When you start to look for courageous people to learn from, be sure to browse through the biography section of your local library or bookstore. Courageous men and women from all circumstances in life have carefully conveyed their inspirations in book form.

Running away, not being present either emotionally or physically, is an old and understandable habit. It is no longer an option in recovery. Being gentle with yourself as you learn to face situations is especially important.

Acting as if you had courage can carry you a long way until the courage itself finds a place in your heart.

I have the courage to change
the way I live.

▼▼▼

It is hard to give up old habits, particularly when you have used them to protect you. You feel a loss when you give them up. For example, some people feel very safe around clutter. They create security nests. Others feel frantic if anything is out of place because their sense of security comes from knowing where everything is at any given moment. However, the quality of your life can suffer if you stay trapped in one of these old habits.

Having the courage to change what you can is a concept familiar to many of you in 12-Step programs. This affirmation will support you in your efforts to make concrete changes in your everyday life.

I have the courage to uncover the past and to own it.

▼▼▼

"Why would anyone want to expose all that pain from the past?" you ask. Those feelings, frozen in place from childhood abuse, have to be felt and released if you are going to heal and live in the present. Otherwise, they sabotage you physically and mentally without your knowing it. Many people, after releasing these feelings, feel physically lighter than they have in years. You may have avoided looking at many areas because you felt ashamed. To do this uncovering takes a lot of courage because it breaks all the family rules, such as "Don't talk" or "Don't feel." Therapy groups and 12-Step programs specifically oriented toward dealing with abuse are safe places to begin.

Grieving over your lost childhood takes time but will little by little put you in touch with your Inner Child. You can begin the self-nurturing that is your ticket to freedom.

Today I acknowledge that I am a courageous person.

▼▼▼

There was no way to acknowledge your courage when you were a child. You did not get praise for being strong enough to live through being beaten, molested, or emotionally blackmailed. Instead, you were ashamed and blamed yourself that these things were part of your everyday life. Today, you deserve commendation for surviving the war zone of your childhood. Many Adult Children actually suffer from Post-Traumatic Stress Syndrome, a syndrome familiarly found in soldiers who have endured combat conditions. The symptoms include insomnia, anxiety, and short-term memory loss. If the battles you had the courage to endure left scars of this nature, there are excellent therapeutic techniques for their treatment today. You can start by seeking professional help.

You have the continuing courage to fight for health and a good life, and you can reinforce your strength each day by acknowledging that you are a courageous person with this affirmation.

You can give yourself positive strokes for the very things you once were ashamed of, a true turnaround for any abused person.

I have the courage to be peaceful.

▼▼▼

The healthier you get, the less you will want to be around desperate people. You will find yourself attracted more and more to people who seem to have an inner peace, and finally, as you seek peace for yourself, you have the courage to truly face your own patterns of being desperate. If you have always been "desperately in love," "desperately worried," or "desperately looking for a job," imagine the opposite, being "peacefully in love," "worried, but still peaceful," or "peacefully looking for a job." Consciously choosing to be peaceful, taking a deep breath, and slowing down whenever the old desperate feelings appear can sufficiently alter the course of your life to bring you into the comfort zone where most people live their lives. It is very hard on your body to go through periods of being desperate, even though you had a great deal of practice in your childhood and are probably good at recovering quickly.

If you focus on being peaceful by saying this affirmation, and you deal gently and calmly with your desperate feelings as they come up, the feelings will diminish over time, and you will find yourself approaching situations from a peaceful point of view.

I have the courage to begin my new life today.

▼▼▼

It is easy to stay stuck in old patterns, particularly if you are trying to make changes in your life without talking them over with someone else. Sometimes, making a commitment out loud to another person can give you the incentive to stick to a plan of action. It is possible for you to borrow another person's courage just for a while until your own courage kicks in. Your best friend may approach recovery with a courage that you admire. Ask others to share their courage with you. Reach out for all the support that you need as you begin your new life. Sometimes you can rely on your Higher Power to give you the courage to continue the search within yourself for your own truth.

The kind of courage that is required to search the darkest parts of your past life in order to clean house for your present life is there for you. If you start your new life of recovery today, you may soon find you are filled with the courage that you never knew was available.

DECISIONS

▼▼▼

You are making decisions all the time. Even when you think you are doing nothing, you are often making a decision. By sitting at home and not getting out to exercise, you have made a decision not to take care of your body that day. By not voting, either in a political contest or an election at school or work, you may be helping someone to get into office whose policies may not be beneficial to you. Everything you do requires a conscious or unconscious decision, and the more you are aware of your own decisions, the sooner you can make more positive choices for yourself. Many of the choices you have made in the past were done in consideration of other people: would they approve, would you offend them, or should you place what they wanted to do before what you wanted to do? Decisions are important to your recovery. You may find the following affirmations helpful in improving your decision making.

I have the power to decide what I want in my life.

▼▼▼

Although most children don't have a great deal of real power in their lives, many of them are given opportunities to make important choices that you might not have been offered when you were growing up. Many children are given choices about which school they want to attend, what sport they wish to play, and which extracurricular activities they wish to participate in. You, on the other hand, may have been ordered to go to your father's alma mater, join the Glee Club because he did, and go out for swimming rather than the debate team because you were expected to follow in your father's footsteps. By now, you have probably realized this constitutes total denial of who you are as a person and is, in fact, severe emotional abuse. Having the power to decide what *you* want in your life means that you have only to deal with your own, not your parents', limitations. It's a new game, learning just who you are and what you really can do, and it may turn out quite differently from the script your family wrote for you.

Acknowledging to yourself that *you* have the power to decide what is in your best interests is a liberating way to free yourself from the past.

I am careful and deliberate in making new decisions.

▼▼▼

Because you were probably not allowed to make your own decisions in the logical way that occurs in healthy families, you may have developed a very erratic method of coping with those few chances you had to try things out for yourself. Many Adult Children are very impulsive in their decision making. They *have* to do something instantly because if they stop and think, it might not happen. The consequences of impulsive decision making can be finding yourself in an inappropriate personal relationship, with a purchase you wish you hadn't made, or on a last-minute trip with inadequate arrangements.

Being careful and deliberate in making new decisions may mean that you discuss each decision with a friend, sponsor, or therapist so that you are forced to take your time, explain everything step by step, and see exactly what you are doing. Although you may believe that successful people decide everything on their own, very capable people consult others frequently before making decisions.

Becoming careful and deliberate and allowing someone else into your decision making process can remarkably improve the quality of your life. You will gain the self-confidence and self-esteem that were lacking in your past.

I stay centered and trust my new decisions.

▼▼▼

If you aren't used to making decisions for your own benefit, you may feel uncomfortable at first. It has been easier for you in the past to accompany others in their decisions, because you were trained to do that from childhood. In households where the parents do not have boundaries, they abusively project their own desires onto their children. As an Adult Child, you have made the decision to look for support outside your family of origin. Staying centered and believing in yourself during this initial breaking-away process is very important. A wonderful book by Gay Hendricks and Russel Wills called *The Centering Book* provides helpful guidelines on how to accomplish centering; the most important one is "Keep breathing!"

If you stay centered, it will be much easier for you to trust your new decisions, especially in the face of resistance from others. Because you have been careful in making your decisions, and because you have reached out for new support, you can trust and believe in yourself.

I take responsibility for making
my decisions.

▼▼▼

One of the payoffs of letting others make your decisions has been to avoid responsibility for what went wrong. It was always someone else's fault. This is a bit like being in prison, where someone else holds the key to your life. When you firmly begin to take responsibility for the consequences of your decisions, you suddenly have a real investment in the decisions you are making, as well as in decisions others are making that will affect your life. Instead of complaining about the poor decision that your brother might have made in choosing a car for you, as you may have done in the past, you now actively participate in choosing the car yourself so that you get what you want. Perhaps you might ask your brother to be there to help you with the negotiations if he is more experienced, but the ultimate responsibility will be yours.

We do not escape the consequences of the decisions we make in our lives. What happens to us happens, and feeling you can blame someone else doesn't really help.

If you use this affirmation and start occupying the central position in your own life by taking responsibility, then whatever happens, good or bad, will be much more satisfying.

**My decisions can be less than
perfect; the important thing is that
I make them.**

▼▼▼

Much of the time, you may have been too frightened to make your own decisions because they seemed less than perfect to your family or friends. Your parents argued with you, and it was too overwhelming to fight for your own way. Gradually you withdrew from making decisions that were independent, deferring to others in order to please them or to avoid an argument. Right now, you may not have much practice or skill at making decisions, but you need to start today by making small decisions on your own behalf. Maybe you have let another person make decisions about the kinds of clothes you've been wearing, thinking that it really didn't matter to you as long as it made the other person happy. Maybe you gave up eating meat because an important new friend was a vegetarian and you wanted to be accepted by her or him. Maybe you gave up playing golf because your family complained it took too much of your time, but you really miss it. Go out this week and do something for yourself: buy a new outfit, eat food you really like, or play a sport that you had given up to please someone else.

Learning to make decisions to please yourself will greatly add to your enjoyment in life. By making more decisions on your own behalf, you can feel much more solid as a person.

When I feel uncomfortable about making a decision, I can take time to weigh the alternatives.

▼▼▼

Giving yourself enough time to make a sound decision that is truly on your own behalf is a strong step toward taking good care of yourself. By taking a little more time to research your purchase of a car, a washing machine, or especially a house, you can avoid making a hasty decision you may regret afterward.

In every area of your life where you have to make decisions, there will be other people with an interest in what you are going to do because it affects their well-being. They may try to pressure you. It will be a sign of growth for you to stand firm, and take the time you need without yielding to gain their approval.

In some instances, *not* making a decision is a valid alternative. You can always make a new decision at a later time.

For chronic procrastinators, this affirmation is not *carte blanche* to postpone your life, but rather a chance for you to realistically look at your decision-making process. It might be wise to set a time limit for each decision with a promise to yourself that you will take your considered course of action when that time arrives.

Now that you are in touch with yourself, at times you may feel discomfort when you are making decisions on your own behalf. This affirmation can help you weather that discomfort and weigh your alternatives, preventing impulsive, spur-of-the-moment decisions. Ultimately, it is our decisions that frame our lives. Changing your decision-making process can have a profound impact on your life.

I make decisions and follow through with them.

▼▼▼

"Into action" is a familiar slogan in 12-Step programs, but consider what it means for you personally. Taking responsibility for your own recovery means deciding on a specific 12-Step program or course of therapy. And following through with that decision means actually attending a meeting or participating in your chosen course of therapy. If you haven't taken that action yet, it is all right to start today. It is never too late to improve your life, even if you feel you have waited too long. One of the stumbling blocks that Adult Children frequently experience is hesitation about taking that first step of reaching out for help. Once you have made the decision to recover, you might take the "appropriate action" by reaching out. Without that action, your decisions have no real meaning in your life.

By following through with action, you can make your decisions the turning points for your future. Repeating this affirmation each time you make a decision will remind you that following through is equally as important as making the decision.

I make my decisions firmly based
in reality today.

▼▼▼

Abused children are forced to somehow escape the hideous reality of their home lives in order to survive. You may have become a master of fantasy, a skill that kept you alive during those terrible years, but this skill works against you now in effectively conducting your present life. Things are happening all around you, and you push an escape button in your head and go off into your own world. You have no idea how much reality you may miss when you go on any given fantasy trip. You may be making decisions with incomplete information because you escaped the present moment. Because you were forced to block out so much negative information from abusive parents, you could now be blocking out information about people you meet which could help you make wise self-protective decisions about them.

Learning how to check reality in order to make sound decisions means communicating and getting feedback from people that you know care about you, who want nothing from you except your growth. These can be the people in your 12-Step program or therapy group, longstanding friends, and your minister, priest, or rabbi. As you grow in recovery, your ability to see what is real and what is influenced by your abusive childhood will become stronger. Things get so much easier when you know that reality is the only game in town, and you become determined to base your life on it.

I capably participate in all decisions in my life, no matter how big or how small.

▼▼▼

Abusive parents rarely let their children make independent decisions. A large measure of emotional, physical and sexual abuse involves their control over you. Allowing you to take part in any decision that would enable you to develop independently would not be in their best interests. As a result, you have often thought that you just weren't capable of deciding things. Unfortunately, feeling this way makes you easy prey for so-called friendly experts who, in the guise of helping you make wiser decisions, will help themselves to your money, your talent, your friends, and anything else that is on their agenda.

When you take responsibility and participate in your own decisions with your own agenda, it becomes less and less possible for others to take advantage of you. While you will still want to seek wise counsel from people you respect, the blind surrendering to another person's wishes will become a thing of the past. When you select a new car with advice only from your significant other, and when you choose a new haircut because you feel it is flattering, not because you want to please someone else, you will notice the difference in the way you feel about yourself.

Everything in your life, big and small, is deserving of your decision-making ability, and you will begin to feel that it is *your* life after all.

Applying this affirmation can improve your relationships in one day. Suddenly, everyone, including you, knows where they stand.

EXPRESSING YOURSELF

▼▼▼

When the house rules you grew up with included "Don't talk" and "Don't tell the truth," expressing yourself was not part of your verbal or emotional vocabulary. If your father gave you a black eye, you told everyone that you fell. Even though you were hurt and angry about being hit, you could never admit it.

When you are not allowed to talk about your feelings, you deny them. You tell yourself or let other people tell you that you feel something else. You will probably want to start expressing yourself in a very safe place, such as a therapy or 12-Step group or in a one-on-one situation. It takes practice to match the words you say to the feelings you have inside when you have not been allowed to do so before. The following affirmations will give you support as you begin connecting your ability to express yourself with who you really are.

I express myself clearly and effectively.

▼▼▼

Imagine how your voice will sound if it is solid and clear and says exactly what you want it to say. After years of not being allowed to talk or being afraid to say the truth because it might offend another person, developing the ability to express yourself clearly and effectively will take practice. You can start by practicing with your close friends. Tell them that you want to make a positive change and need their support. By asking for their help ahead of time, you don't run the risk of catching them off guard and perhaps having them reject your new way of handling yourself. It is part of speaking effectively to plan ahead and create situations that work for you.

Repeating this affirmation out loud as you are walking around your living room or driving in your car will help change your beliefs about your ability to express yourself. If you believe that you can speak clearly and effectively, you will be supporting all your efforts to do so. Your work on this will suddenly be so much easier, and you will be able to handle many situations in your life with greater effectiveness.

I ask for what I want easily and appropriately.

▼▼▼

As an Adult Child, you were so often used to anticipating and fulfilling the needs of your parents that you assume everyone has the same ability to "mind read" that you have. You were praised for having dinner ready without being asked and beaten if you didn't. Just to make sure everything went smoothly, you often fixed your father's drink and served it before he had a chance to complain that no one ever did anything for him. One father announced proudly, "Tony is such a wonderful boy. He anticipates my every need." He had no idea what a crippling relationship he was describing.

You learned to mind read to get love and approval and many times to make sure you didn't get physically harmed. You assume others were taught to operate in the same way, and therefore you don't know how to ask for what you want. This can lead to frustration and anger with your friends or spouse when they don't do what you expect them to do. From now on, assume that *no one* can anticipate your needs, not your spouse, your children, your best friend, or your coworkers. Start asking easily and appropriately for what you want and watch how quickly your frustration level goes down. The anxiety level of your friends and family will be much lower also, as they will no longer have to live up to unexpressed expectations.

I can comfortably express to
others how I feel.

▼▼▼

Suppressing feelings is extremely common for anyone who has been abused as a child. Your parents took up all the space with their feelings. Your feelings were not allowed, and so they went underground. In recovery, after you have done the work of getting in touch with your feelings and learned to process them for yourself, the next step is to learn to be comfortable in expressing those feelings to others.

Maybe you were never allowed to say you were tired or hungry when you were a child. It will be a new experience to say to a friend, "I'm hungry. Let's stop at the store. I'd like some fruit." Or, "I'm feeling too tired to go to the movies tonight. I'll take a rain check."

Congratulate yourself on your courage in taking these steps. They will lead you to the emotional freedom to be yourself.

I feel confident speaking in front of groups.

▼▼▼

Many recovering people meet in therapy groups or in 12-Step programs to share their experiences and gain emotional support. The people who receive the most benefits from being part of such groups are the ones who share their feelings. This affirmation will help you become one of those people who contributes most to your own recovery.

Once you feel confident in sharing your feelings in front of your therapy or 12-Step group, you will be astonished at how much easier it is to make a presentation at work or in front of an organization you are involved in. Giving yourself the gift of self-assurance has wonderful benefits that extend into every area of your life.

I express my anger responsibly in positive ways while addressing old pain from my childhood.

▼▼▼

Talking your anger out with a friend or therapist is a good way to deal with it, rather than imitating the yelling and tantrum-throwing that may have gone on in your house when you were a child. You probably have an enormous amount of rage stored up from your childhood that you need to deal with, perhaps in an anger workshop or one-on-one with a therapist. Anger that isn't dealt with always comes out in direct or indirect ways.

You know now that there are alternatives to your old angry behavior, that you don't have to act on every feeling you have, that you don't have to overreact to your spouse or your coworkers. You have choices. If you think that you are going to "lose it," you can take deep breaths, excuse yourself, and make a phone call to talk to a friend. You can go for a walk in the woods or on the beach, or even yell in your car (when it is safely parked).

If you deal with your anger responsibly and positively, you will be addressing and healing the old pain from your childhood.

When I express myself, I improve and maintain my physical health.

▼▼▼

When you internalize your feelings, especially anger, you can cause your body damage that may show up in the form of a physical disease or disability. In Adult Children who were abused and had to keep their mouths shut in order to receive any amount of attention from their parents, no matter how small, migraine headaches, chronic fatigue syndrome (CFS), low back problems, and even cancer are not uncommon. Marilyn, who suffered from Epstein-Barr virus and Candida, went into therapy to deal with her anger and completely recovered from those diseases after two years. Yet there are people who have suffered for as long as 10 years without much relief. They have never dealt with their inability to express their emotions.

If you have any kind of chronic health problem, take a look at whether you have been avoiding feelings all your life. Co-Dependents Anonymous, Al-Anon, or therapeutic groups that specialize in helping Adult Children from abusive families are safe places to explore learning to express your feelings. You can also ask a sponsor or therapist what expressing your feelings appropriately means.

This affirmation brings with it the possibility of renewed physical health. Say it often and begin expressing yourself today. The physical benefits will be gratifying.

When I feel affection for someone,
I now express it.

▼▼▼

Expressing affection isn't easy when you have been abused; the lack of trust and the fear of rejection get in the way. Expressing affection appropriately is a normal, healthy way for people to relate to one another. Telling others that you enjoy their company is an appropriate step toward becoming better friends.

Sometimes, when you've had a wonderful time taking a hike in the woods, playing chess, or seeing a movie, it may be appropriate to give a good-bye hug if you are sensitive to the other person's receptiveness. An arm-around-the-shoulder hug is a good, gentle way to start. It's non-threatening, and the other person is free to respond or withdraw if he or she wishes. Expressing your affection for others helps form stronger friendship bonds.

Although you have old fears about rejection, taking risks by expressing your affection is well worth it. Friendships can only become deeper when people know that they are appreciated. If someone chooses to shy away from your expression of affection, you can reevaluate the relationship. You can commend yourself for growth and courage in an area that will add much richness to your life.

I enjoy expressing myself creatively.

▼▼▼

Giving yourself permission to be creative is one of the nicest things you can do for yourself. Since everyone is unique, the ways in which you express your creativity can be personal and rewarding to you. Your creative expression could be in the way you arrange the furniture in your house, in the special spices you add to your spaghetti sauce, or in the way you dress. Being creative isn't limited to people who paint, write, or play music. You can appreciate the flair you have for conversation or the way you've planted the flowers in your garden. The choices are yours, so express yourself!

FEELINGS

▼▼▼

Experiencing your feelings and being able to talk about them were certainly against the rules in your abusive household. Unfortunately, in our society expressing your feelings openly is often not accepted in many places, such as at a corporate or civil service job, in the bank when you discover a major error, or at school when dealing with your child's teacher. In these situations it is definitely more effective to contain your feelings. But for Adult Children who have been abused, there is a deeper problem. Many times you won't even know what you are feeling. You have to learn to identify what it is you are feeling in each situation.

When you begin to realize that you are feeling an emotion, find out which of these four basic categories it falls into: sad, mad, glad, or scared. Ashamed and lonely fall under the category of sad; angry and resentful are varieties of mad; comfortable and passionate are shades of glad; and afraid and tense are classified under scared. There are many other words that describe gradations of basic feelings. You can read about feelings in recovery literature or ask your friends how they would feel under circumstances that you are experiencing. The affirmations on feelings will help you become aware through practice of what your feelings are. When you know what you feel, you will have a choice about what action you will take on your own behalf.

I acknowledge and responsibly release feelings that come from my past.

▼▼▼

People brought up in a nurturing, healthy environment got support from their families in expressing their emotions as they came up. In your family, living with an abusive parent, you learned that expressing your feelings was dangerous and provoked abuse, and that it was safer to pretend they didn't exist.

To acknowledge your feelings, you must pause from time to time and pay attention to what your body is experiencing. Are there areas of tension in your shoulders or jaw? By practicing paying attention to your emotional state, you will begin to notice sensations and emotions.

Now that you are grown and away from your family situation, there may be many years of feelings you have repressed that need to be acknowledged. One way to tell if this is true is if you find yourself overreacting to present situations. See if you can find a pattern running through your overreactions that you can trace to your childhood. What was the original transaction between you and your parents that caused the pain you have repressed? John Bradshaw talks about the necessity of feeling that original pain, working through it, doing your grieving, and then releasing it. Many people are able to do this in a responsible way in their 12-Step program or in therapeutic workshops where a safe environment is created. You may choose to work one-on-one with a safe person of your choice. This is powerful, wonderful work that is life-changing when you do it. Use this affirmation to support you throughout this liberating, life-affirming process.

I acknowledge that all my feelings are OK.

▼▼▼

Many of your feelings were probably not OK around your family. Your anger and your joy were particularly difficult for them to take because it meant they weren't able to control you. As you begin to really feel for the first time in your life, all those forbidden feelings will start to surface. Now, as an adult, you can tell yourself that it is OK to feel whatever you feel, but you can also make responsible choices about how you act on those feelings. Alex was told by his mother, "Don't whine and cry, or I'll give you something to cry about!" Alex felt it wasn't OK for him to feel angry or sad. He stuffed away those feelings until very recently. Now each time he feels the anger or sadness that was originally forbidden to him, he writes about it and what it means to have it in his life. Keeping a journal of your feelings, acknowledging that all of them are OK to feel, is one way to support your growing individuality and separation from those old family beliefs.

It helps to tell yourself every day on paper that what you feel is OK.

It's OK for me to be angry with people who try to manipulate me.

▼▼▼

When you were constantly manipulated as a small child by the emotional needs of your parents, it was completely unsafe for you to be angry with the outrageous use they were making of your time, energy, and emotions. You had to continue to live their lives. After all, they were all that you had for your survival.

Patricia has had a very hard time even recognizing manipulators. Her training to deny their ways of operating was deeply ingrained in her when she was very small. On the occasions when her mother rejected him, her father sought refuge in Patricia's bed. She was sexually abused for 10 years by a charming con man who called her "Daddy's girl" and said he loved her more than anyone in the world. She is now learning that love does not mean allowing someone to abuse her body while saying "I love you" and that it is healthy to be angry as soon as she detects this.

Most manipulations are more subtle than the one I just described. But you can save yourself a great deal of pain by learning to watch other people, listen carefully to what they are saying, and recognize that any anger you start to feel may be a warning that you need to acknowledge and then act on.

Because I feel more sure of myself, I can comfortably deal with other people's emotions.

▼▼▼

As you become more sure of yourself and stop being afraid of experiencing your own feelings, you will lose the tendency to shut down or overreact when other people express themselves intensely. Your knowledge of your own boundaries helps you to feel safe in situations that used to trigger anxiety. If you had a raging parent, it is a great relief to be quietly detached around someone else's rage. The world can be a comfortable place when other people's emotions don't throw you completely off, when you can feel sure about your feelings in the face of someone else unloading his or her own.

When you are sure of yourself, you can stay calm in everyone else's storms.

I act on my feelings in constructive
and reasonable ways.

▼▼▼

There are certain children who grow up playing the central role of rebel and scapegoat in the dynamics of their abusive households. If you played this role, you are probably carrying a lot of anger which you have acted out in the past. You were the child who ran away from home, who fought back and expressed the wrongfulness and helplessness that others in the family felt, and who broke through your denial and called attention to the fact that there was something wrong in your family. You risked punishment for being honest and speaking out and only brought more abusive treatment on yourself.

If you continue this role as an adult, it becomes increasingly painful because your outbursts can affect your job, your friendships, and your relationship with society. What was once your survival behavior can leave you feeling lonely and isolated. Leaving the role of the rebel behind means being willing to deal with your frustration and anger in constructive ways by helping others less fortunate than you, writing in a journal every day, or exercising regularly. It also means developing the ability to contain your feelings until you are in a safe place to decide what to do about them. Although the world is certainly not a fair place, those of you with the courage to speak out often suffer the most at the hands of those whose injustices you would like to stop. There are constructive and careful ways that you can appropriately speak out and make your feelings known.

It is worthwhile to reconsider a new life and a new point of view by handling your feelings constructively and reasonably.

I enjoy my good feelings today.

▼▼▼

One of the heartbreaks in listening to Adult Children over the years is hearing how their parents extinguished their normal childhood joys one by one—the thrill of finding a bird's nest or a bluejay's brightly colored feather, for example—and replaced them with the abuse of the moment.

When you give yourself permission today to be ecstatic even for a few moments, you are thawing the deep emotional freeze imposed on you by your parents. "Normal" people are nurtured by small things that give them great joy—a card from a faraway friend, or a beautiful seashell found in the sand. Feeling the joy and expressing it can be very healing.

If you find it difficult to enjoy fantastic experiences because you are so shut down, be gentle with yourself. You are injured, and you can heal. By beginning to feel and express all your emotions, your ability to enjoy and appreciate will continue to grow.

When I feel destructive feelings, I ask for help.

▼▼▼

Taking contrary action is a recommended method for dealing with negative feelings. It never used to be all right for you to tell anyone when you felt bad, and it certainly was not all right to ask for help. That would mean someone outside your family would find out the truth. You were forced to handle all that negativity alone and it often meant acting out those feelings with addictions. Therapy groups and 12-Step programs are filled with people who were not allowed to tell anyone how much they were hurting. Prisons house those who chose criminal action to deal with their feelings instead of getting help.

When Mary's husband spent all their savings on cocaine and took off for Canada, she knew she was capable of buying a gun and handing him his ticket to heaven. When she told her therapist that she literally "wanted to kill him," the therapist helped her understand and process her rage so that an actual murderous action was never a real possibility.

Give yourself permission today to call one of your friends or even a hot line if things get really bad and there is no one else available. When you come from an abusive family, sometimes you feel that you will explode if you don't act on your feelings. That belief can change as you explore your options. The intensity of your feelings will diminish when you begin to really process them. Asking for help is the first and most important step in the healing process.

I have the courage to defend
my feelings.

▼▼▼

How often have you heard, "You shouldn't feel that way. You have no reason to feel badly." When Scott's Aunt Louise died last week, a well-meaning person told him, "You shouldn't be sad. She was so lucky to have died quickly. It could have been a whole lot worse, don't you think?" The person was trying to make herself feel better at the expense of Scott, who was truly grieving for the aunt who was closest to him. By gently telling people, "You know, I am really sad. She was the closest to me of anyone and I will miss her terribly" defends your right to have your feelings without discounting the other person.

When you allow others to take away your feelings without acknowledging your right to have them, you diminish your self-esteem and sense of self. Now that you are recovering from serious overt abuse, it is good to be aware that there are other kinds of abuse that are damaging but much less obvious. Whatever feelings you have are yours to process.

Acknowledging and defending your feelings is part of becoming the confident, whole person that you are working toward.

FORGIVENESS

▼▼▼

It has been said that to understand is to forgive. In order to understand, you must allow yourself to feel the repressed anger and hurt that you have been carrying around toward your parents and others who may have abused you. In *For Your Own Good*, Alice Miller wrote, "Genuine forgiveness does not deny anger but faces it head-on. If I can feel outrage at the injustice I have suffered, can recognize my persecution as such, and can acknowledge and hate my persecutor for what he or she has done, only then will the way to forgiveness be open to me."

If you are not ready to forgive your abusers, then don't. Save that step for last. What's most important anyway is to forgive yourself. When you can fully experience the outrage and the pain that you have stored from your past, you will most likely begin to feel some compassion and understanding. It is obvious that parents who abuse their children were themselves abused. They were too frightened to face their own anger and hurt, so they perpetuated the abuse onto the next generation. You are breaking that chain of fear by facing your rage, feeling it, expressing it, and letting it go. The process of forgiveness that you are pursuing is painful, but it is well worth the rewards. Acknowledge yourself for your courage.

I am willing to go through the process
of forgiveness.

▼▼▼

In the reality of coming to terms with abusive parents, forgiveness is more than a simple one-step process. The pain you have suffered was so great that forgiving has to begin with the realization that holding onto these feelings is seriously harming you. Letting go and forgiving offers the possibilities of a whole life. Hanging on could mean continuing misery and poor health.

Being willing to go through the process of forgiveness means that you are choosing life and the opportunities of the moment rather than being right or punishing your abusive parents. This is a very different step for you. The process of changing the way you think about your parents, seeing them also as damaged children who grew up into adults physically but remained small children emotionally, is part of the process. It allows you the freedom to let go without wanting revenge, because revenge against a damaged person brings no satisfaction and can only cause you more pain.

Holding onto past resentments cripples the possibility for love, whereas forgiveness opens the doors for you to experience yourself as a warm and loving person. This is the powerful first step in the process of forgiveness.

Being willing to forgive is the necessary bridge between your hatred in the past and your hope for love in the present and future.

I forgive myself for being available for abuse.

▼▼▼

One of the most difficult things about being abused by your parents is forgiving yourself for what you envision as "letting it happen." When you were a child and your parents behaved in an abusive way, stop to think what a terrible dilemma you faced. If you stood up and tried to say "Stop!," you took the risk of cutting off the only source of "love" and physical support available to you. If you challenged your parents' behavior and were rejected, maybe you would be sent away or abused again. You felt you might die if you took that step of standing up to them.

Think about how hard it is today for you and others you know to deal with these issues as an adult, to stand up for yourself in an abusive relationship even when you have a support group and friends. When you were small and had no one, it was truly impossible.

If you can give yourself the forgiveness that comes from the understanding that you did the only thing you could do, to survive, you can move forward on the path to healing and the rest of your life.

I forgive myself for not choosing myself and my well-being first.

▼▼▼

What you can choose freely for yourself today in no way resembles the abuse you had to accept in the past. When you were growing up, you didn't have a choice about your well-being. The adults around you made those choices for you, and if they had to use you for their own needs, your well-being was forgotten.

If you have continued to sacrifice yourself for the lives and pleasures of others now that you are an Adult Child, you will recognize this pattern from your childhood. By understanding what happened, you can forgive yourself for not learning about boundaries and for being unable, until this point, to put your own welfare first.

You are free now to start developing those boundaries and making those choices for yourself.

I forgive myself for all the anger and pain I have held onto.

▼▼▼

Holding all that anger and hurt inside may have given you a sense of comfort over the years and may have been the force behind your continuing survival. But as time goes on, harboring bitter resentments and wanting to get even can harm your growth emotionally and spiritually and can actually do damage to your physical health. It is time to forgive yourself for doing the best you could by hanging onto that anger and using it as an energy source.

If you can actually reexperience those original feelings of pain and abuse in a safe place for you—a workshop or group, for example—they can be transformed into sorrow and compassion. When you forgive yourself for all the feelings that you clung to in order to survive and let go of the negative side of your anger, your resentments will finally lift and you will feel much, much lighter.

Forgiving yourself is an important key to your recovery.

I forgive my abuser for pushing me beyond my innocence.

▼▼▼

Whether you suffered emotional, physical, or sexual abuse, you were a substitute, a stand-in, for an adult who was unwilling to endure what you were forced to take. You were pushed in every instance into roles that were entirely inappropriate for your age.

Rose's mother was an alcoholic who frequently took to her bed or went to stay with her own father, who lived nearby, in order to recover from her latest ailment. At age 10, Rose learned to cook for her father, also an alcoholic, and three younger siblings. She was 11 when the youngest child was born, and she took charge of the baby. Rose was nearly running the entire house at 13, a surrogate mother to the younger children and a surrogate spouse to her father, who abused her physically and sexually.

Losing her innocence meant that Rose continued to take care of men and rescue others until a friend took her to a Co-Dependents Anonymous meeting. There Rose learned about caretaking and rescuing and slowly stopped doing them in her life.

Rose does have enormous grief for giving so much of her life inappropriately to other people and for being forced to become an adult from the time she was 11 years old. But by working through her grief and focusing on living in the present moment and forgiving her parents, Rose has improved the quality of her life more than she could have imagined.

When you have lost your innocence and never had a childhood, you have a lot of catching up to do. Now is the time to start.

I forgive my abuser his or her need to find love in such a harmful way.

▼▼▼

It is difficult to acknowledge that much of the abuse of your childhood was a pathetic way for one or both of your parents to find some form of love or power for themselves. If one parent is abusive toward the other, the parent on the receiving end transfers the abuse to someone small in order to feel good about himself or herself. It is an unforgivable situation that you must find the strength and the heart to forgive in order to get on with your life.

Gary was the victim of his father's brutal criticism and his mother's physical violence. He had nowhere to turn when he was a child except to the family cat, Figaro. He sometimes talked to Figaro for hours. His father and mother divorced when Gary was 20 years old, and the tension was broken. Gary established a surface relationship with both parents and a stronger relationship with a good therapist. He was able to forgive and detach from his mother before she died, and today does what he can to be supportive of his father, who has diabetes. Gary has detached successfully from his father's criticism and keeps his own life very strong and very separate from his father's. He understands today that his father's criticism came from his frustration with Gary's mother, and that has made it easier for Gary to forgive him.

It is easier to forgive when you don't take the abuse personally.

I forgive myself for not knowing about boundaries.

▼▼▼

How can you know about boundaries when you were in a family where no one had any boundaries, where you were not given a chance when you began to say "no" in your first attempt to become separate from your mother. Instead, your mother punished you for being a bad child. You were never allowed to develop any boundaries or sense of self because your family system could not have continued as it was if you had done so. No one dared to be a real person in your family because it might draw attention or abuse.

You need to congratulate yourself for surviving that family and finding the tools for your recovery. There was no way for you to learn about boundaries until now, so it makes sense to forgive yourself.

You form the strongest boundaries when you have a foundation of forgiveness.

I forgive myself for not knowing how to help myself.

▼▼▼

One of the things to watch out for as you enter this recovery process is questioning why you couldn't have done better much earlier in your life. If you make it very hard on yourself for what you didn't do, you will miss the wonderful opportunity you have created for yourself to grow and change.

Michelle continues to beat herself up over the fact that she should have known to go for help when her father beat and sexually abused her 40 years ago. This destructive hindsight kills the spirit of the recovering person. All the shoulda's, woulda's, coulda's were not possible when you were a child trapped inside a completely abusive, dysfunctional family.

Michelle forgets to ask herself, "Where could a 10-year-old turn 40 years ago under such circumstances?" She compares herself to the women of today who are protected by child abuse laws that did not exist when she was a child. She can grieve today over what happened to her and feel enormous sadness that all the children of her generation who were abused did not have any protection or any adults who were bound by law to report such aberrations. Later, if she feels it would help her growth and healing, she can join an activist group to protect today's children against such abuse. Beating yourself up is an old habit that all of us need to leave behind.

Changing your self-talk from negative to positive can help greatly in the forgiveness process. Being compassionate to yourself is necessary before you can forgive anyone else.

When I see my abusive parents, I forgive them and see them as small children calling out for love.

▼▼▼

One of the gifts of recovery is the ability to no longer take things personally. We can detach and see our parents as very needy children who require our help. When Nick's mother was in her 70s and became ill with emphysema, she lost her will to live and overdosed on sleeping medication twice in four months. Nick's brother threatened to institutionalize her because he couldn't deal with her, and she called Nick in a panic to come help her.

Nick had suffered terrible emotional abuse from his mother throughout his childhood. Whenever Nick did anything his mother did not approve of, she refused to speak to him for months at a time. But when Nick saw his mother in poor physical shape, very depressed and very childlike, he was able to detach and be a compassionate, competent adult, making all the necessary arrangements for his mother's admittance to a safe and comfortable retirement hotel.

After spending many hours helping his mother get settled and often holding her because she was frightened, Nick was totally surprised to hear her say quite abruptly, "I'm sorry for all the awful things I did to you. I feel terrible about it, and I want you to know that I really love you. I just didn't know what to do with you." And she started to cry. Nick put his arm around her and said, "It's okay, mother. I'm doing fine. You know it's really been up to me for a long time anyhow.".

When you take responsibility for your actions, it becomes easier to forgive your parents' actions.

FRIENDSHIP

▼▼▼

Telling yourself that you don't need anyone, that you can make it alone, robs you of the support and love that you now need because you did not get it as a child. Friends are wonderful to share your life with—the joyous times you can reminisce about in years to come, and the heartbreaking times when a friend's hug can make you feel like forging ahead in seemingly unbearable situations.

Many of you have found making friends difficult. You didn't learn much about friendship from your abusive parents. Skills for building friendships *can* be learned: being there for another person by actively listening to what he or she is saying and being a sounding board, or sharing activities that you enjoy with another person. Friendship is one of the many benefits of moving beyond survival and affirming your life.

I continually reach out to make new friends.

▼▼▼

The more people you meet, the more likely you are to make new friends. It is important to practice reaching out during this growing-up-again phase. Some of the people you meet may turn into valuable friends.

Learning to trust people is an important part of this development, but it may happen slowly. As you gain more confidence in trusting your own instincts, you will be able to tell more easily who it is safe to trust. Your expectations will be more realistic about what friendships are, always changing, evolving, and growing, and some of the changes come as a result of resolving differences rather than running from the conflict. You will feel comfortable and happy in your friendships when you welcome the change rather than denying it or avoiding it.

I attract loving and supportive friends.

▼▼▼

If you have come to expect abusive treatment from others as the result of your childhood, you may feel uncomfortable at first around kind and loving people. But underneath your own defenses is a warm and loving person who deserves caring, committed relationships.

As you remain honest with yourself about your need to be involved with others, and as you move slowly to develop your trust and lessen your discomfort, such friendships will come into your life. But staying home doesn't put you in the traffic pattern. You have to make the effort to get to groups and activities where there will be people who share your interests. By taking that step forward, people can appreciate you for who you are today.

I feel comfortable in altering my behavior with my friends.

▼▼▼

Feeling safe enough to change your behavior with a friend, trusting that he or she will still be there for you, is a new experience, especially if you grew up in a family where you had to take care of others to feel accepted. Now that you no longer want to be a caretaker, you can set specific limits on your willingness to be responsible for others. For example, if you have allowed yourself to become a "taxi service" that is costing you valuable time and money, start limiting your availability. You can say, "I won't be able to drive you to work on Monday. I have another appointment."

It may feel very uncomfortable to honor yourself over someone else's needs, but with practice, it becomes much easier. And worthwhile friendships will survive the changes you are making.

**I spend relaxed and joyful leisure time
with my friends.**

▼▼▼

Sharing leisure activities with friends who also enjoy these activities is part of having a happy, fulfilled life. You can have different friends who like different activities. Some friends may enjoy going to the museum with you. Others may like to go sailing with you. Still others, such as your tennis partner, may not like either museums or sailing. Enjoying what each individual has to offer you is a wonderful relief from the all-or-nothing way of thinking that many abused children learn from their parents. Having just one common interest can create a bond from which a deeper, long-lasting friendship can develop.

I share my real self with my friends.

▼▼▼

Learning to be your real self, first with yourself and then with your friends, is the reward for putting boundaries in your life. When you learn that you are OK after all and that to have people enjoy your company doesn't require that you take care of or please them, you have stepped over an invisible threshold into a mansion of possibilities.

Sharing information about yourself and your feelings strengthens your self-confidence. When you share who you really are and people are accepting and supportive, you feel wonderful.

I am a good friend.

▼▼▼

This may be a new experience for you, practicing the skills of friendship and being a good friend. Offering your undivided attention to a friend, being willing to listen without offering advice or criticism, is something that no one may have ever given to you as a child. It is a special gift that you can give to another person. The ability to listen closely and actively means that you effectively communicate. You can paraphrase the content of what your friend is saying by restating his or her ideas or by interpreting his or her feelings. This way, they know exactly what you understood and can correct any wrong impressions.

It will take practice to learn to listen this way. Remove any judgments about doing it "perfectly." Give yourself credit for making the effort and enjoy watching your friends respond in a new way.

I love and accept my friends exactly as they are.

▼▼▼

When you criticize yourself each time you make a mistake, it is inevitable that you set those same standards for your friends, standards of perfectionism you learned from highly critical and nonaccepting parents. To begin loving and accepting your friends, you need to begin loving and accepting yourself. Put yourself at the top of your list of friends. Give the best beginning friendship to yourself and quality friendships with others will feel much more natural. If you accept your own mistakes and forgive yourself generously, it will be much easier to do the same with your friends.

By loving and accepting your friends, you will know that the mistakes they make are not a betrayal intended to harm you, but rather normal human behavior that is part of everyday life. And if something happens between you, you can talk it over openly and honestly and work things out.

I give my friends healthy support when they are going through difficult times.

▼▼▼

Sometimes, when people start a recovery program by trying to take care of themselves, they aren't secure about the concepts of boundaries and rescuing. Rather than taking a risk, they go overboard by being overprotective of themselves, and they temporarily forget the value of friendship in their lives.

A good rule of thumb: You don't do something for others that they could easily do for themselves. However, if a friend of yours is nine months pregnant and not feeling strong enough to go to the market one day, the healthy supportive act of friendship is to do her marketing for her if it does not harm you in the process—that is, if it doesn't threaten your job or conflict with some urgent priority in your own family that must take precedent.

No one can make it alone. We all need support and friendship, but if you are used to rescuing others and allowing yourself to be abused by others, it is valuable to monitor yourself and your boundaries during the process of regaining your own self. Just be sure you understand that caring for other people is still an integral part of your life. You simply make yourself aware, set limits, and give healthy support to your friends whenever you can.

GRATITUDE

▼▼▼

Cultivating an "attitude of gratitude" is exactly that: cultivation. It is neither a gift from the universe nor something you were instantly struck with, like a lightning bolt, but a thoughtful process that takes awareness and effort. Dwelling on your own misery was understandable for you when you were a child and could not escape from your living situation. Also, you were not allowed to talk about your difficulties, so you had no feedback and no frame of reference. You could not imagine anyone having a harder time than you were having.

Today, if you reach out by sharing in a group with others who have suffered as you have, you may gain an entirely different perspective. Listening to someone who has far more serious difficulties than you ever faced, who deals with them courageously, can help you see that you have much to be grateful for. By talking to others and ending your isolation, you can become more aware of all the things there are in the world for you to take advantage of. You can feel grateful to be alive, to have survived the horrors of your childhood. The following affirmations are designed to help you strengthen your concept of gratitude and make it part of your life each day.

Being grateful for my gains is a good way to keep them.

▼▼▼

The chaos of your dysfunctional family didn't offer many opportunities for gratitude. Children learn to be grateful from the attitudes of their parents, from a belief system that values taking the time to appreciate all that you have. In your family, those quiet, reflective times were few, if any. When you became an adult and started providing good things for yourself, it never seemed safe to stop and be grateful. Perhaps you might miss the next opportunity, or you might lose what you have already if you slow down for even a minute. This is an illusion.

Taking time to say thank-you to the universe for allowing you to enjoy the good things in your life creates the attitude that will allow you to encourage more good to come into your life. Living in fear on an imaginary treadmill creates stress and possible ill health if carried to the extreme. This attitude of gratitude, which is cultivated in 12-Step programs, works on your behalf. By appreciating the gains you have made in your life and enjoying the moment that you are in right now, you can move forward to greater gains with cheerfulness and confidence.

I overcome self-pity with gratitude for all the good I have in my life.

▼▼▼

Self-pity seems to be a major by-product of growing up as an abused child. Almost everyone seems to suffer from it to some degree and has to work at keeping it out of their emotional repertoire. Whenever you catch yourself stumbling back into the cesspool of self-pity, try making an instant "grateful list." This technique has been suggested by many spiritual disciplines and is recommended regularly in 12-Step programs. Concentrating on what you don't have will not bear any fruit, only frustration. Looking at the advantages you do have with the idea of developing their potential can reap many rewards.

When you begin to build on the solid foundation of what you do have and then value that foundation, things can definitely change for the better in your life.

Being grateful today for what you've taken for granted in the past puts sunshine in your life in all those places where you had allowed only darkness.

I am grateful to my Higher Power in my prayers and meditation for all the good that is in my life today.

▼▼▼

You are probably used to crying out for God's help during your darkest times, ready to change your life if only your prayer to get out of this particular jam were answered. Your prayers have obviously been answered over and over during your lifetime because you are here and looking for a better way to live. Gratitude cleanses the spirit and is a soothing, healing agent, particularly when you are feeling troubled.

Cultivating gratitude, thanking your Higher Power for all the good in your life today, completely shifts your energy into a different gear, and you find that you can all of a sudden take a positive action that a short time ago seemed beyond your willingness and ability.

I am grateful for positive teachers in
my life who believe in me.

▼▼▼

Somehow you got from your childhood to where you are
right now. You did not only survive but believed enough
in yourself today to reach out for more information about
how to overcome the suffering of your childhood. There
were people who believed in you, and it is strengthening for
you to affirm that.

Perhaps it was your second-grade teacher who told you
that you were very talented and should study painting. Now
you are a graphic artist, having overcome the total disapproval of your family, who can't understand anyone being
involved with the "impractical arts." Or maybe it was your
coach who convinced your parents to let you play in Little
League and provided all your transportation himself because
your parents weren't about to put themselves out for an
extracurricular activity. Or maybe it was the high school
guidance counselor who told you you were college material
and helped you fill out scholarship applications because your
parents couldn't afford your tuition. Now you've gone on
to graduate school and plan on becoming a teacher just
because someone cared and believed in you when your
parents didn't.

Remembering with gratitude those important people who
were there for you changes the complexion of your life
somewhat. It wasn't *all* black even then, and today there
really are some wonderful people in the world if you just
leave yourself open to the opportunities and let them into
your life when they come along.

I am grateful for the peacefulness of nature, and I let it nurture me.

▼▼▼

The peacefulness of nature is a direct opposite to the abusive home you came from. As a child, perhaps you sought refuge in a nearby park or woodland, or if you lived near the ocean, you may have made daily pilgrimages to the beach to think things through or to escape from your parents' fury. Perhaps you didn't even have those kinds of opportunities when you were a child and, as a result, don't know much about appreciating what nature can do for you. Now is the time to find much of the peace and nurturing you need in nature.

If you are adventurous, you can begin to explore possibilities yourself. Check newspapers or magazines at the library to find out what beautiful areas are close to where you live. Many cities have beautiful, peaceful parks that are truly a refuge during a lunch hour or at the end of busy workdays. If you like organized activities, the Sierra Club and the Audubon Society offer supervised nature hikes and weekends in the wilderness.

Taking the time to look at flowers, to watch birds and butterflies, will slow your entire body down into reasonable relaxation. Since relaxation was not part of your childhood, it's important that you give it to yourself now and let your body get the rhythmic rest it needs to stay balanced.

After you have received this wonderful nurturing from nature, gratitude is definitely next on the agenda. It is with deep appreciation and gratitude that you can gain the full benefit of your experiences.

I am grateful for every kindness in my life.

▼▼▼

The many years you lived without kindness in your family may have left you so unfamiliar with real kindness that you feel uncomfortable when someone offers it to you. It may seem at first like the manipulation your mother used when she wanted you to behave well in front of company so that your family would look "normal." But the act was over once the company left, and the truly kind people in your life today don't change character to create effects. In fact, they seem to care more about giving you a hand than any reward for themselves.

Gradually, as you reach out to more and more people, you will find a number of them are thoughtful, considerate, and constructive. Learn to accept and appreciate their kindness.

I am grateful for my ability to give and receive.

▼▼▼

When you were locked inside your own fear, participating in healthy exchanges with other people was out of your reach. If someone gave to you, you wondered immediately, "What does she want?" You were afraid to receive because you knew there were strings attached, and, given your surroundings, you were right. Maybe you learned from your role models and became a compulsive giver, hoping to bribe people into loving you and doing what you wanted, none of which came from genuine giving.

All of that has changed now that you are an adult and on your own. You can choose your friends and they can choose you on the basis of mutual interests and enjoying one another's company. You can get to know people and practice giving a different way, giving of yourself rather than buying something. Invite a friend over for dinner, finding out ahead of time what he likes to eat. Then cook something special just for him. Offer to baby-sit or pet-sit for friends so that they can get away without having to pay dearly for it. Consider doing volunteer work for a nonprofit organization that you believe in. Helping others is an integral part of healthy giving.

Being willing to let go and receive the generosity of others is often more difficult than learning to give, because in receiving you become vulnerable. If you are reluctant to give up control, this is a big step. Allowing yourself to receive with appreciation can give you a good idea of how much of what you do for others is appreciated. It is wonderful for your self-worth. You have joined in meaningful honest exchanges with other caring people. You are no longer alone.

I am grateful for my ability to communicate clearly.

▼▼▼

When you were forced to keep secrets all during your childhood and were not allowed to say how you felt or what was real for you, your ability to communicate clearly and directly was literally suffocated. Today, you are learning not only who you are, but how to communicate your knowledge honestly to other people. In 12-Step meetings, people are allowed to share for three to five minutes without interruption and without fear of being overwhelmed by criticism of their every opinion. The opportunity to talk from one's own point of view for that length of time helps strengthen many people and helps each person develop his or her own sense of self.

Developing your own sense of self and communicating clearly from that new, strong place inside you changes the way you are perceived by others and can make a tremendous difference in the quality of your interactions.

Affirming your gratitude each day for the opportunities you have will encourage you to use those opportunities for your continued growth.

HEALING

▼▼▼

When you have been abused as a child, there is frequently deep, old pain that can no longer be contained. It surfaces involuntarily in your dreams or in unexplained illnesses. If left unexamined, this pain can wreak havoc on your health, your relationships, and the quality of your life.

Healing from the abuse of your childhood *is* possible, but you have to commit yourself to your healing plan and follow through with it. Today, there are many routes to choose from, including self-help groups, body work, hypnotherapy, acupuncture, and other emotional-release techniques. Whatever healing techniques are most effective for you are the ones you can use to best advantage. Just because your best friend found one-on-one therapy most effective for him does not mean that it will work for you. Each of us finds our own way.

These affirmations will strengthen whatever avenue of healing you choose, and because you can use them wherever you are, they can give you support during the day when you are by yourself. Affirmations are a statement of faith, and faith is of prime importance in healing.

Every day I become more and more healthy.

▼▼▼

Denial rises up, especially in life-threatening illnesses and in cases of severe sexual abuse where dealing with the issues feels just as life threatening. But if you want to live a healthy life, there comes a time when you must face the truth about your past abuse and make decisions about what action you are going to take. In some cases, by talking about your issues and taking responsibility for yourself as you are today, you can start moving in the direction of becoming healthier almost immediately. There are miracles that have occurred when people release their pain and begin a program of self-love.

If your battle for health is less dramatic—you are getting by, functioning fairly well without making a huge effort to deal with childhood abuse—you may need more encouragement to raise the level of health in your life because you are tempted to let things stay as they are. Reach out for support and encouragement from other people who are in recovery and ask them what they are doing to help themselves.

Learning from other people is a wise way to become healthy. If you want to get healthier every day, you need to start somewhere, and learning this new affirmation is a good place.

My healing makes way for my feeling more love and more compassion.

▼▼▼

When you were unwilling to consider the process of healing, your rage was helping you continue to survive. Now the rage is harming you physically and emotionally, and it is time for you to make room for more love and more compassion in your life.

If you are diagnosed with a disorder that is greatly aggravated by stress, such as rheumatoid arthritis or heart disease, your doctor may recommend that you go into therapy to work on your anger. If you have never addressed your anger at your abusive parents, this might be the right time to do so. Some of us need permission to begin to take care of ourselves, and a doctor's orders can be the wakeup call we need.

After some months of therapy, you will probably find that your whole attitude has changed and that you have what is known as a new lease on life. If you were a tough, stoic Adult Child, you may find yourself filled with compassion and gratitude that are totally different from any feelings you have ever felt.

We all have enormous room for healing and love in our lives if we are willing to let go of our anger and resentment.

I allow a sense of peace to come over me as I let go of the pain.

▼▼▼

When you come from an abusive household, letting go and surrendering are totally foreign concepts to you. You only know how to fight, either overtly or with passive resistance.

Deborah didn't know how to rest or pace herself. As an environmental attorney, there was no end to the cases she could take, but they did not pay particularly well, so in order to manage financially, she undertook too many cases. Eventually she became run down and developed walking pneumonia. Still she would not stop. Finally, once Deborah was in the hospital, a friend convinced her that she had to change. When Deborah made the decision to let go of the pain in her chest and the pain in her life, she felt incredibly peaceful for the first time in her life.

After she was discharged, Deborah changed her law practice to include consultations to environmental companies in the area of hazardous-waste liabilities. These consultations paid well, and she was able to keep her hours manageable and take care of her health.

Letting go of physical pain can often lead to a general letting go in your life and a peacefulness that you never dreamed of.

I believe that I am a miracle.

▼▼▼

Because you are so interested in life that you reach out for recovery and look for affirmations that will help you find your way through your pain, you are a miracle. You have survived deprivation and abuse and you still care about living. You have probably already stopped whatever addictions could have masked your pain, which in itself is remarkable, and now you are left with the pain itself and looking for some help to deal with it. Using these affirmations will give you continuing support, but you will also need to search out other help that feels comfortable to you.

Telling yourself every day that you are a miracle keeps the positive energy flowing. If you go to therapy or a support group, you will find other people like yourself who have miraculously survived the journey and are growing, changing, and becoming healed of their childhood pain.

Miracles are possible. Look in the mirror every morning and you will see one.

My sense of humor helps me heal
more quickly.

▼▼▼

Keeping your sense of humor no matter what befalls you is an element in the healing process that has only recently been medically documented.

A wonderful man, Norman Cousins, was diagnosed with a degenerative disease of the connective tissues, a fatal illness. He convinced his doctors to let him try radical "laugh" therapy and megavitamins. He moved into a hotel and rented old comedy movies—the Marx Brothers, the Honeymooners, and others. Miraculously, he recovered from his illness and went on to lecture all over the world on the value of humor in healing.

If your pain is emotional pain from your childhood, humor is remarkably effective in putting everything into perspective and letting you move back into the present moment from your painful past.

Humor is a wonderful friend and a powerful healer.

I am willing to take the time to heal gradually from the pain of my childhood.

▼▼▼

When you begin the work of recovery, you hope that you will overcome the pain of your childhood right away. Unfortunately, the work of recovery takes time. When Chuck first entered Co-Dependents Anonymous, he thought that he would be "fixed" in a few weeks. What he found instead was that healing is a slow process. During that process he looked at his childhood, discovered what happened, and discarded his illusions. After two years in CoDA, Chuck's life was much happier. He had boundaries for the first time in his personal life, and he was developing a relationship with a woman that felt secure.

If we take our time, the healing process will take its time.

I cooperate with my own healing by taking good care of myself.

When you are healing from the abuse of your childhood, you need to take good care of yourself. Facing the pain can be very tiring, and it is necessary to get plenty of rest and recreation to balance the pain.

Sam is in therapy to deal with the physical abuse that he suffered from his mother. To balance what he is doing in psychotherapy, Sam works out at the gym three nights a week after work. He says it gives him the strength to continue his psychological healing.

Healing can happen more quickly when you support it with your entire self—mental and physical.

I am able to be healthy and self-loving when faced with difficulties.

▼▼▼

By changing your attitudes toward yourself and maintaining self-love in the face of difficulties instead of your previous self-critical behavior, you can continue your growth toward healing.

It is easy to be healthy and self-loving when things are going well. When something unexpected goes wrong in your life, then your attitude becomes much more difficult. Melissa had been the manager of a museum gift shop for two years. She had had a tough time bringing the small store back from the brink where it had slid due to previous poor management, but she was doing quite well and proud of herself for the shop's attractiveness and quality merchandise. However, the board of directors was not convinced that the store could stay out of debt permanently and wasn't willing to take the financial risk to let Melissa prove that it could be done. They gave her 60 days to close the store and become a mail-order–only outlet.

At first Melissa was angry at their shortsightedness, but as she gained perspective, she saw it as an opening in her life to do something she had always wanted to do—go to law school. Melissa really loves herself, and no matter what happens in her exterior life, she will find a way to make it a healthy and positive experience.

Healing is also keeping a healthy attitude.

LEARNING TO COMMUNICATE

▼▼▼

A difficult task for most of us who come from abusive households is learning how to communicate in a way that is effective. The confusing communication that we grew up with, filled with secrets, dishonesty, and paranoia, left us unable to get what we wanted in life because we really did not know how to ask. What all of us have learned in recovery is to own our own feelings, because without that crucial emotional step, our communication cannot be ours. We are left asking questions to please others instead of making choices for ourselves.

The following affirmations can begin your work on improving your communication. Clear communication involves changing your thinking, which in turn has a powerful effect on your feelings.

Learning to communicate well, to be genuinely assertive in taking care of yourself, can make a world of difference in the effectiveness of your life.

I am learning to ask for what I want.

▼▼▼

In abusive households, children learn quickly that it is wrong to ask directly for what they want. Michael learned when he was five years old that if he asked for what he wanted, he would certainly not get it. Because his directness was rewarded with outright refusal, he soon learned not to ask directly anymore. Instead, he learned to barter. If he took the dog out for a walk for an entire week, then he could go to the movies.

Michael was given confusing messages from his family which he carried with him until he got into recovery. He learned that you never get what you ask for, so you have to trade favors for what you want.

This convoluted communication gave him difficulty at work. He wasn't able to be direct with his superiors or his fellow workers. By finally addressing his communication problems in a workshop, Michael learned to ask for what he wanted directly, with good results. The people at his office respected him more than when he was trying to manipulate them into giving him what he wanted, and he didn't have to trade his time and energy to get something he could simply ask for straightforwardly.

If your questions are direct, you have a good chance of getting what you want.

I can communicate clearly and concisely today.

▼▼▼

Your difficulty in communicating stems from the behavior you witnessed in your family. When Laura was growing up, she noticed that her parents never talked with each other, they talked *at* each other. Everyone in her family told long, rambling stories. After he had his nightly martinis, her grandfather told stories about the good old days. No one was allowed to interrupt or ask questions, even though they had heard the same story over and over. There was no communication.

Her parents looked at each other and made superficial conversation, but Laura could tell there was no connection between them. Her father often yelled at her mother, so Laura understood that her mother did not feel safe when she talked with him.

Now that Laura has left home, she is making an effort to have real conversations with people. By observing other people who have a communication style that she admires, Laura is learning to improve her own skills.

When you can communicate clearly, others respond to you in much more positive ways.

I now act in ways that communicate the person I am today.

▼▼▼

When you have grown up in hysterical surroundings, it is understandable that you might behave hysterically on occasion. Unfortunately, until you learn to change your behavior, you present yourself to the world in a way that does not represent who you are today.

Learning how to act appropriately is very important, and the wisest place to look for advice is a trusted friend. It is good to cultivate friendships with several people with whom you can be completely open. You can also turn to self-help books, including those on etiquette, and start to trust your instincts about your behavior which are becoming increasingly dependable in recovery. Changing your behavior after so many years may seem like a difficult task. But if you clearly communicate to others all the new things you have learned about boundaries, forgiveness, and taking care of yourself, you will be acting in ways that communicate who you are today, and responses to you will be remarkably different.

If you communicate clearly, you have a much better chance of being the person you really are.

I am listening to myself and
honoring what I hear.

▼▼▼

Listening to other people is a specialty of children from abusive families. Listening to other people's voices inside your head has been a primary preoccupation of yours. Learning how to listen to your real self is a basic communication skill that you were never taught because you were always listening to your abusive parents. It is a skill that takes practice and time.

Allison had never even thought about listening to herself until she joined a therapy group. Most of the other people in her group had been in groups before and were used to raising their hands and speaking directly about their feelings and about other people in the group. Allison began to practice listening to herself about how she felt before raising her hand.

Sometimes she would make a comment to herself on what someone else said. Then she noticed her own voice wanting to speak on issues important to her. Slowly, she got in touch with that voice and began to speak clearly on her own behalf. The group provided her with a safe place to learn a new skill.

You have to learn to listen to yourself before you can act on what you hear.

I can communicate intimate feelings.

▼▼▼

It is a wonderful privilege to become close to another human being and to share intimate feelings. Sometimes it takes a long time because we stopped communicating any intimate feelings from the time we closed down as children. Shutting down a child's potential for honesty and intimacy happens regularly in an emotionally abusive household. It takes work and good fortune to learn to communicate those intimate feelings when you are an adult.

When Raymond began his recovery, he started to talk about feelings for the first time since he was a small boy. At that time his mother had told him that men don't show their feelings. Raymond believed her for many years. Today, Raymond is married and works hard to communicate intimate feelings to his wife. They are both committed to a caring relationship. They affirm their ability to communicate intimate feelings to each other.

Sharing intimate feelings is the graduate course in learning to communicate.

LETTING GO

▼▼▼

After many years of being abused, part of taking care of yourself is learning to let go. When enmeshment with other people, places, and things has been a way of life for you, your first steps toward letting go and establishing your own priorities may seem lonely and not very meaningful. You have run everyone else's races and rescued other people from their pain because that was what you were taught.

David was the oldest of four children. His parents were alcoholics whose violent fights often ended with both of them injured and requiring care. David bandaged them when he could and called the family doctor when one of them was badly hurt. The police had long since stopped responding to their domestic difficulties. Whenever possible, he kept the younger children upstairs, shielded from the outrageous behavior of their parents. Recently, David discovered that he was taking care of people inappropriately and taking very little care of himself. He started working the Co-Dependents Anonymous Program and letting go of old behaviors and people who were not healthy for him.

The following affirmations can put you in touch with areas in your life where letting go could benefit your health and well-being.

I let go of my desire to be perfect.

▼▼▼

This is such a big letting go. The desire to be perfect has most likely been with you ever since you were able to walk. You probably wanted to walk perfectly after that first step in order to get the approval of your parents. You need to please others and want their approval, two age-old non-antidotes when you think you are not enough. Doing or saying something that "they" disapprove of, whoever the current parent-substitutes are in your life, feels like a life-and-death choice because the "you" that you think you are might literally be killed off by their disapproval. There would be nothing left. So your desire to be perfect seems absolutely necessary because it is an integral part of that life-or-death struggle.

The transformation from this desire into a more balanced, confident life happens gradually as soon as you have your own boundaries and feel self-contained. You begin to sense that you are indeed enough. The giant hole inside you starts to fill in. Since you have become your own separate individual, no one's approval means life or death for you. The only approval that you require is your own, and you can consciously choose to be loving and generous with yourself. At long last, you can let go of the desire to be perfect.

After careful consideration, I let go of friendships that stand in the way of my growth.

▼▼▼

Before you began your recovery, you may have had certain friendships that you kept because of mutual interest or the length of time you had invested in them, even though they did not support the new attitudes and actions you were taking in your life. Now that you are healthier, you can feel your friends' need to control you by wanting you to stay as you were, neatly fitting into their lives. It is time to let go.

During this period of growth, you may have started a friendship only to find that the person you befriended has turned out to be quite different now that you know him or her better. Perhaps he or she is very controlling now that they feel safe, or wants much more of your time than you wish to give, and is demanding about it. Give yourself permission to let go of these kinds of relationships that don't work well in your life any longer.

To let go, after careful consideration, means that no one has to be at fault, that you will choose to grow naturally into other relationships.

Today, I let go of fear. I breathe deeply and relax.

▼▼▼

It was impossible not to be afraid in an abusive household. Fear has become a constant companion for you, a habit that you are holding onto even though it no longer has a useful purpose in your life. You are an adult now, free from the physical circumstances that caused your original terror.

Janice wasn't even aware that it was fear she constantly felt. She thought that was the way she always felt until she took a yoga class and was taught how to breathe deeply from her stomach. Miraculously, the feelings of tightness that had her literally by the throat disappeared while she was breathing. It is physiologically impossible to hold onto fear if you are engaged in deep breathing. Learning yoga or relaxation techniques can help you release the fear you have carried in your body since you were a child.

Your whole attitude and outlook on life can change when you start letting go of the fear you have stored since childhood.

I let go of my resentments toward other people and events.

▼▼▼

When you were small, did you ever harbor the secret thought that when you grew up, you would get even? It was hard not to feel this way because even if you didn't have any power over your parents when you were a child, the future was on your side. You would get big enough eventually to fight back if you wanted to. That way of thinking can become an addictive habit. You use it today as a reason to delay taking positive action when things haven't gone your way. "Someday," you say, "when the time is right, I'll get even." You fail to take responsibility for your own actions.

The book *Alcoholics Anonymous* cautions that resentment is the number-one killer of alcoholics, and that if you are an alcoholic, you cannot afford resentment because it will ultimately cause you to be so unhappy you might drink. This advice is just as true for people with other addictive patterns. Hanging onto resentments long enough will almost surely trigger your addictions.

Letting go of resentments involves looking at the reality of what's happened and acknowledging that you are the one suffering now by holding onto the injury of being rejected or betrayed, and that in the grander scheme of your life, this too shall pass. If an asteroid crashed into the earth tomorrow, would this resentment make a difference? Letting go is the most constructive way to deal with resentments.

I let go of my desire to control other people's behavior.

▼▼▼

When you were growing up, you told yourself a myth that if you could just control the behavior of all the people in your house, you would be safe. Of course, you never had a chance to prove that this myth wasn't true, because your chance to be the ruling power never came. But you've been trying ever since you left home to make it happen.

News flash—reality. You can only control your own behavior. You can control your reactions to other people's behavior, but you cannot control their behavior. Controlling your reactions is the way to ultimately feel the safety you wanted in your childhood. If you feel strong and centered inside, you can stay calm in the face of other people's behavior and react well regardless of how difficult the situation becomes.

Letting go of the hopeless desire to control the behavior of others leaves you with more contentment and more energy to live your own life.

I release my past and live in the present.

▼▼▼

Many people live a large portion of their lives in fantasy about events—the time they went to the Senior Prom, or how, in college, they drank more than anyone else on campus. Your old resentments are not the only memories that negatively affect you today. Too much time ruminating on the past, good or ill, doesn't help you focus on and find solutions for your current problems.

If you find yourself continually lost in fantasy, there are centering techniques to help bring you back into reality. These simple but effective techniques include breathing deeply from your stomach, grounding yourself while seated by rubbing the soles of your feet back and forth along the floor, and wearing a rubber band on your wrist and snapping it to bring you back to center.

Living your life in the present is a challenge for all Adult Children who have been abused, because we are such excellent mental-escape artists—it was our survival tool. Becoming aware of your thought patterns, pulling yourself back, and "being here now" gets easier with practice. Tell your Inner Self with this affirmation that you are committed to living in the present.

I let go of obsessive thinking.

▼▼▼

Feeling that something isn't right in their lives is a common complaint of abused Adult Children. One way to avoid dealing with the reality of whatever is bothering you is choosing to obsess about a person or situation. By thinking obsessively, you avoid your feelings in the present. You become entirely focused on something outside yourself and your current problems. When you catch yourself doing this, you can actively *let go*. Turn your palms up, open your hands, and relax them. Just this physical symbol of letting go can often break the obsessive thinking long enough to allow you to bring your focus back to what you need to do today. One of the 12-Step program slogans is "Turn It Over," which means turning whatever is bothering you over to the care of your Higher Power, thereby breaking the power you have let a person or situation have over you.

Try monitoring yourself. If you find that you are spending far too much time concentrating your thinking on one person or situation, do everything you can to let go and come back to center, to yourself.

I let go of the need for chaos in my life.

▼▼▼

Chaos can be an old habit, a familiar security blanket from childhood that we drag around with us everywhere we go. The chaos can be in our surroundings, in our personal relationships, in the way we organize (or don't organize) our time, or in the way we approach our work.

Although Sharon hasn't lived at home in her family's chaos for 20 years, even today she feels uncomfortable if things are in any real order. The quality of her present life is suffering because she hasn't let go of her childhood habits. She can't find anything when she wants to. She wastes a great deal of time looking for her keys, the scissors, or a certain pot in which to cook dinner. This is a direct repetition of the way her family lived. Everything was in visual chaos all the time, so Sharon feels insecure if everything is neat and where it should be. What she is working on today is keeping things neater around her house by picking up at the end of each day. Whenever she does a real cleaning and has the whole place in order at one time, Sharon tells herself that she lives in a safe and beautiful space that is nurturing to her. She is gradually desensitizing herself to the old feelings of discomfort that she experiences around order. She is beginning to feel comfortable for longer and longer periods of time without having to resort to the familiarity of chaos in her home.

You can accomplish this in any area of your life where you cultivate chaos. Slowly allow yourself to experience the lack of chaos for longer and longer periods of time. Letting go of chaos *can* be done gradually. Make a slow transition into a way of conducting your daily activities that will support all the healthy changes you are bringing into your life.

I let go of my need for drama
in my life.

▼▼▼

While growing up, the drama in your house was real. Your father really did chase your mother with a carving knife, and you did tackle him in the kitchen to save her life, or you endured something similar over and over. What developed was an addiction to the adrenaline that comes with the kind of drama that is continuously repeated in front of you until you don't feel *really* alive without that kind of adrenaline rush.

In the present, you keep reacting intensely in situations where intensity is inappropriate, or you create drama whereas another person would take things step by step in a calm manner. For you, a minor rear-end collision balloons into a dramatic event in which you might have been severely injured if your car hadn't had such a good bumper. Everything becomes more important when drama is added.

To let go of your drama means that you must first become aware of how much it affects your body, your relationships, and your reactions. Then, see if you are willing to change your approach to all the experiences in your life, to take things peacefully and not be swept into making more of everything than there actually is. Doing a lot of deep breathing helps keep the intensity at a minimum.

Breaking the addiction to your own adrenaline requires the same caring attention that is required to deal with any addiction. Many people in Co-Dependents Anonymous are working on this particular process addiction, and you might find support in those groups to help you through the initial stages of recovery. The rewards for your body alone make letting go of the drama a vital part of your recovery.

LOVE

▼▼▼

L earning to really love is one of the big tasks in the process of recovery. Many of you may have received unconditional love from people outside your immediate family, perhaps from grandparents, aunts and uncles, friends, or teachers. However, the major distortions about love—for example, that pain and abuse equal love—which you suffered from your permanent caregivers take hard work and reeducation to overcome. The love you are learning about in your recovery has no strings attached, is not manipulative, and is there for you in spite of anything you might do.

The 12-Step programs tell newcomers to "Let us love you until you can love yourself." You can learn a lot about how wonderful you are by letting other people love you. Loving yourself is a gradual process of working through your pain, accepting yourself as you are, and being willing to give yourself the kindness that you have been giving to others all your life. Love is what all of us from abusive families had too little of. Now you can make up for lost time.

I express love easily and joyfully.

▼▼▼

Staying frozen in the feelings of the past can rob you and others of all the love you have to give. This affirmation can help you overcome the fear of expressing love to the people close to you. You can write a poem, paint a picture, or buy a small bouquet of flowers as ways of expressing your love to them. Or best of all, you can hug the person you love and say "I love you" easily and joyfully.

I love my Inner Child unconditionally.

▼▼▼

All children need unconditional love early in their development. With that kind of love, they become secure and develop into emotionally strong adults. If you were not fortunate enough to have a parent capable of giving you unconditional love, you have an option. You can choose to be your own healthy parent and give your Inner Child the unconditional love it needs to grow and allow you to get on with your life.

There are many books that are helpful with this process. John Pollard's *Self-Parenting* and John Bradshaw's *Homecoming* discuss techniques for working with your Inner Child. It's a big job to reach inside yourself and discover the hurt and pain your Inner Child is suffering and then take responsibility for dealing with the hurt, but the feeling of wholeness that develops from taking this time to care for your Inner Child makes the work incredibly valuable and rewarding.

I remove all obstacles to loving myself completely.

▼▼▼

Growing up with parents who took out their rage and frustration on you turned you completely backward when it came to loving yourself. You want love so badly that you think getting it from other people at any price will fill the emptiness inside you. You can remove that obstacle to loving yourself by realizing that there will never be enough love from others to fill you up. Let go of the belief that others are the source from which you can draw love for yourself. Being willing to experience yourself exactly the way you are, letting go of illusions and the need to please others, moves you into a world that can truly work on your behalf, a world in which you can love yourself completely.

I love myself through whatever experience I am having.

▼▼▼

If you believe that you can love yourself only when you are having what you consider a healthy or loving experience, you are missing the whole point of what really loving yourself is all about. What if you have taken your anger out at someone at work who didn't deserve it because you were really mad at your wife or husband? Under those circumstances you will definitely need more love and compassion for yourself than when you have done something particularly loving and generous. You will need to give yourself solid support rather than a congratulatory pat on the back in order to feel strong enough to properly apologize and get yourself centered again.

Loving yourself at the times when you feel least worthy of being loved can give you the strength to pick yourself up and start over again. Self-love provides wonderful flexibility to absorb the hard knocks. It is no longer necessary to add insult to injury by topping off a bad experience with a round of self-destructive acting out. When you are 100 percent on your own team through all kinds of experiences, good and bad, you truly reap the benefits of loving yourself.

The more love I share today, the more love I am open to tomorrow.

▼▼▼

If you share love today, your pathways to more love are automatically opened. Loving takes practice at first, especially when love has never been a regular part of your life. If you feel afraid that by giving more and more love you will be giving yourself away, guess what? It is just the opposite. The more love you share with others, the more you actually fill your own cup.

One of the mistaken beliefs of many children from abusive families is that they have been so damaged they have nothing to give to anyone else. This belief needs to be dispelled right away. When you have suffered in your life, you have so much experience on which to draw. You can empathize with the pain of others because you have truly suffered yourself. There is no phoniness when you say, "I understand. I have been there," and the person you wish to love and help can tell immediately you are speaking the truth.

The more love you give today, the more you keep your pump primed for tomorrow. Giving and being open to receive love can be a wonderful new habit in your life.

I am willing to make healthy compromises to maintain love in my life.

▼▼▼

Being stubborn and refusing to compromise may well be behavior that your parents paraded in front of you when you were growing up. It is impossible to maintain any kind of love or close relationship when those qualities dominate the people involved. Kelly had a mother who simply stopped talking to anyone who disagreed with her until he or she either came around to her way of thinking or left her life permanently. This kind of banishment was a pitifully effective form of bribery and domination.

She didn't speak to Kelly for several years when Kelly chose to live with a man her mother didn't like. This mother once locked her own husband out of the house for a month when he refused to accompany her on a trip. Needless to say, with this kind of outrageous tyrannical model, Kelly was terrified to even try negotiating because it had never worked in her experience. She started out slowly by negotiating with friends who she had come to trust on things like what movie to see or where to have dinner. In so doing, Kelly built up her skills and courage and now does well for herself in more important arenas—with her supervisor at work, and with men on dates, for example.

Realizing that the world is not a replica of your family situation can help you break out of the behavior modes that you never thought you could break.

You can maintain love in your life and nurture relationships that have always been "mysteriously" destroyed before. There really is a whole new world out there as you make your way toward recovery.

ONE DAY AT A TIME

▼▼▼

As a child, you focused far ahead into the future, to the time when you would be free of your abusive family and on your own. You developed this way of thinking to help you endure those very hard times. There was little advantage to mentally remain in the abusive present when you were a child, because you had no power to change your circumstances.

Now, however, that same ability to escape into the future prevents you from enjoying present time and from seeing your circumstances exactly as they are so that you can take positive action for yourself. All that we really can do physically is to live one day at a time, and many of us have to make a conscious effort to live that way.

These affirmations can help keep new ways of thinking always present.

One day at a time, I open my heart.

▼▼▼

Love is a rainbow of good things: compassion, sharing, and things that come to you by giving and opening up your heart to others. Experiencing real love is likely to be new to you since you began to recover from your childhood abuse. Many of us confuse our impulses to be generous with real love, and unfortunately those impulses are part of the rescue syndrome that we learned in our abusive families. Once we are able to see our patterns, however, we can enjoy the wonderful parts of ourselves that are truly loving.

Maria worked as a fund-raiser at a shelter for homeless women and children. One day, another worker brought her three-year-old grandchild to visit, and the little girl climbed right into Maria's lap and declared her affection. When Maria learned that the child's mother had abandoned her in favor of drugs and alcohol, Maria opened her heart to the child, and they have been friends now for four years. Maria takes her to the zoo and the movies, buys her birthday gifts, and last year tutored her in reading. Opening her heart to this child has given Maria compassion for the devastation that abandonment causes in a child. The grandmother is grateful as well to have another adult to help enrich the child's life.

Opening your heart on a daily basis can open your life.

One day at a time, I comfortably accept unexpected situations.

▼▼▼

When you are perpetually off balance from the trauma you carry with you from childhood, it is unsettling to deal with unexpected situations in your life. It is harder for you than it is for the average person to deal with an uninvited guest for dinner or a dent you find in your car. The unfortunate consequence of dealing with your life in such a narrow margin is that you are uncomfortable too much of the time. Each time something newly unexpected comes along, you may have not yet recovered from the last one.

As you work through your recovery program, you will begin to feel less frightened and more comfortable about living in general. You might want to look at what special fears come up for you during unexpected situations. How do these fears parallel what happened when you were a child? When we examine our fears and find out the beliefs that lie behind them, those beliefs often have nothing to do with our present lives.

When we examine the things we do, we often find that there isn't a good reason for us to continue doing them.

One day at a time, I make amends for my mistakes and keep my life current.

▼▼▼

Whether you came from a hostile camp of grudge holders and resentment carriers who didn't own up to their mistakes, or a very nice family who swept everything under the rug and accepted no responsibility, you had no role models of how to behave when you made mistakes. If your family's behavior was out of line, they often attacked instead of saying they were sorry, or they pretended that it never happened.

One of the biggest changes that you make when you leave your abusive family behind is treating other people with much more consideration, taking responsibility for injuries you cause other people when you make mistakes. When Paul was growing up, he heard a lot of *"I'm* not saying 'I'm sorry' to him," and he got the idea that owning up to your mistakes wasn't necessary. Sadly, many of us have had to unlearn these kinds of lessons. We have had to look for better ways to get along with other people, owning up to your mistakes and making amends so that you can go on with your life comfortably.

Even if you haven't ever admitted you made a mistake before, you can start today and improve your life.

One day at a time, I can deal with the pain from my past.

▼▼▼

If you are afraid to even look into your past because you feel that the pain might be too great for you to handle, this affirmation may give you a way to pursue your recovery in more manageable increments. If you deal with the pain of your childhood one day at a time, and you also provide yourself with positive support while you are doing this work, you may make real progress slowly and be able to stay with it.

Some people feel they need a safe environment such as a workshop designed specifically to explore their original pain and inner child work. These workshops are advertised in the *Sober Times* and other recovery-oriented newspapers. Other people work through this pain with a sponsor or therapist or in 12-Step meetings. It is a time-consuming process, but well worth it.

Looking at your pain in a way that feels safe and comfortable for you is a vital step in your recovery.

One day at a time, I take an inventory of exactly where I am.

▼▼▼

Before we get into recovery, most of us are thoroughly accustomed to self-obsession but not at all used to honest self-appraisal. One of the most effective tools in any recovery program is writing a daily inventory in your journal so that you can accurately assess on the page what has happened during the day and evaluate just where you stood in every transaction. You can also go over your journal entries after two or three weeks to measure your progress.

Brittany wrote the following: "I left for work 10 minutes late, so it seemed like everyone was in my way and holding me up. I made it to work with 30 seconds to spare and was feeling really stressed before I even started working. When one client called asking about a refund, I managed to be civil to him. I see now that I was really grouchy to my coworker Marian right after I finished that call. I'll apologize to her tomorrow so that there won't be any bad feelings. From now on I have to be sure to leave the house on time so that I don't take out my resentment about being rushed on anyone else."

When you put your day down on paper, you have a chance to see everything in perspective and then take action if necessary.

One day at a time, I am willing to ask for help.

▼▼▼

When you have been afraid to ask for anything since you were a child because the consequences might provoke abuse, it may be difficult to realize that, as an adult, it is safe to ask for help when you need it, both personally and professionally.

Jan had spent most of her life as an extremely independent person, even in her marriage. She was very competent, but she never realized the stress she placed on herself by her unwillingness to ask for help. Her husband offered many times, but she always refused. She remembered recently while participating in a workshop that she had been continually insulted by her father for requiring help of any kind. He believed in instant self-sufficiency, so Jan had vowed never to ask for or accept help again. That decision has caused her much hardship.

Today, with her new awareness, Jan has changed her behavior a great deal by asking for help when she needs it and accepting help from her husband when he offers it.

Asking for and accepting help brings us closer to the people we share our lives with.

One day at a time, I make room for
fun and recreation.

▼▼▼

When you work hard during the week, you need to treat yourself to some fun and recreation. It's a chance to spend time with someone you especially care about or to get together with a group of close friends. You can try out different activities with people to see what you like. Some people love the movies and go almost every weekend. Others like outdoor activities. If you are looking for something new to do, look in the calendar section of your local newspaper to find lists of upcoming concerts, dances, lectures, and other activities you may be interested in.

Robert attended a monthly meeting of his local ski club, a social event for skiers in town. An Adult Child, Robert had skied frequently with club members but never felt confident enough to attend any of the club's social events. After several months in a support group, he decided to go in the face of his fears and attend this meeting. Everyone was very friendly at the gathering, and Robert met a woman with whom he seemed to have a lot in common—skiing, of course, as well as a love of hiking, bicycling, and camping. They have been seeing each other ever since. Robert has learned to enjoy himself.

Fun and recreation are good for their own sake, but they also bring a lot of healing to your recovery.

OPPORTUNITIES

▼▼▼

Once you begin recovery, one of the big advantages is the awareness that life has many more possibilities than you thought. As your emotional and spiritual growth continues, you find choices open to you that would never have happened without the work that you are doing.

Many people recovering from abusive childhoods discover that fear has held them back from learning new skills, and they decide to go back to school. Martha spent 20 years in the nursing field and went back to school to get her master's degree in psychology. She moved to a beautiful city in another state and is loving her new life as a family therapist.

The following affirmations can help you discover opportunities in all areas of your life. Perhaps your opportunity lies in the possibility of new relationships or a new career. Whatever it is, you are awake and alive for it!

There is a positive opportunity in everything I experience.

▼▼▼

Everything that we think, say, feel, and hear in our environment each day is an experience. These experiences can be pleasant, unpleasant, or indistinguishable. Unfortunately, when you have abusive parents, you get confused about what you're receiving. Because of your low self-esteem, it's much easier for you to experience negative things than positive things. By paying close attention to your body's reactions to these experiences—sweaty palms, rapid heartbeat, stomachache, and so forth—along with what you are feeling emotionally—fear, anger, or even love—you will begin to see the pattern of how experiences affect you.

Learning to listen to your body can increase your self-awareness, and give you insight into how you respond to a situation and how others respond to you. This process is a positive opportunity that comes from paying attention to how you conduct yourself in everyday activities.

Kate has been observing for two months how she acts in her daily activities. She noticed that she gets very defensive if someone even hints that something she did wasn't good. By taking an honest inventory of herself, Kate discovered that this behavior had prevented her from developing close friendships and even harmed her at work. She started attending a group in which she could safely interact and try new behaviors. She is relieved to be able to acknowledge and deal with what she has been doing for so many years.

Every experience is an opportunity to evaluate where we really are and to decide whether to make changes.

When the opportunity to make amends with people from my past arises, I am comfortable and willing to do it.

▼▼▼

Making amends is often very difficult for Adult Children to do. They were often never shown how in their families, everyone was right all the time, and apologies were not part of the family behavior.

If you grew up in that kind of family, your dealings with people have probably gotten you into lots of trouble. Maybe you borrowed things on occasion without asking because everyone in your family borrowed clothing, tools, or food without a second thought. You didn't realize then that other families lived differently, with boundaries. The friend whose jacket you borrowed two months ago for a hot date is unhappy that you haven't returned it. The neighbor next door wants his rake. There were many of these incidents during your life that you never thought about until you learned the importance of boundaries and began changing your behavior in recovery.

All the people you injured deserve amends, and if you still live in the same town where you caused the harm, you could run into those people anywhere. Now, instead of having to cross the street or hide to avoid them, you can take the opportunity to make amends for the discomfort you caused them long ago. In most cases, people are surprised but grateful that someone would care enough to make amends.

Sometimes people from the past cross your path unexpectedly, and you can take advantage of that opportunity today to take care of old business.

Every day I create opportunities to feel better about myself.

▼▼▼

Learning to expand your vision about opportunities for growth can become a rewarding search. When Valerie finally became committed to her exercise program, she began taking long walks as part of it. In addition to feeling better physically, Valerie became familiar with her neighborhood, admiring the colorful gardens and stopping now and then to appreciate the beautiful flowers and have conversations with the neighbors. After several months, she felt better physically and mentally. She realized that talking with the neighborhood folk was helping her overcome her shyness and fear of strangers, even though her original intention was to gain physical strength and stamina.

If you take the opportunity to feel better about yourself in one area, sometimes you find wonderful benefits in another completely unexpected place.

I feel healthy enough to take risks today and take advantage of opportunities.

▼▼▼

Part of the joy in recovering is the freedom to take risks, perhaps for the first time ever as an adult. When you have had drilled into your mind all the things that you couldn't do, you have to feel healthy enough within yourself to take risks today, to talk back to the voices inside your head that question your new activities.

If you have never participated in a physically adventurous sport and you have always wanted to, you might look into hot-air ballooning in your area or white-water rafting. You might want to save money for the trip of your dreams to Australia or the Far East, something you wouldn't have felt you deserved before committing to your own health.

The opportunities will always be there if we are willing to take risks.

I welcome opportunities to make new friends.

▼▼▼

Things are very different now that you have your own place to live as an adult. The fears about bringing people home because you never knew what to expect are gone, and your home life can now be what you want. If you have created a nice home for yourself, you can use it as an opportunity to make new friends.

Jerry loved his comfortable new apartment, which was within walking distance of the center of the suburb where he lived. He had created a wonderful place to bring friends. It was now up to him to reach out and make the friends. Jerry decided to ask one new person a week to go with him to a movie, on a bike ride, or on a walk, and if he and the person seemed compatible, Jerry would invite him or her another time to his apartment.

Within three months, Jerry had taken advantage of his many opportunities at work to make five new acquaintances who were fast on the way to becoming his friends. He had broken the pattern of his childhood.

Reaching out means taking advantage of opportunities in your own environment to form lasting friendships.

RELATIONSHIPS

▼▼▼

Relationships have their own special rules in each abusive family, but the rules that threaten reality—"Don't talk," "Don't feel," and "Deny everything"—are prevalent among all these families. You weren't supposed to express an unacceptable feeling as a child, and you paid dearly with some form of abuse if you did. In an abusive family, no one deals with his or her feelings in a direct, honest, and caring way. You carry these handicaps in interpersonal skills into your adult relationships today.

To overcome the legacy of denial takes work. Reversing the process of shutting down and learning to remain open to what you are experiencing now is a constant struggle until it becomes an established new pattern and relatively comfortable for you. The following affirmations can help you build new thought patterns and new skills as you develop your ability to have good relationships.

When someone asks too much of me, I can say no and still feel loving toward them.

▼▼▼

If you were taught black-and-white rules of operating with people when you were a child, this concept will be a real growth step for you. Saying no is not a contradiction to loving someone and continuing a good relationship with them. In fact, the ability to set limits is essential in maintaining loving relationships.

If you have a friend who always has to choose the movie or the restaurant, you feel uncomfortable that you have no say in these decisions now that you are developing boundaries. You like your friend and want to continue to see her, so it makes sense to try to work it out. For years you have wanted this friend's approval, so you didn't make waves over her arrangements. Now that you are healthier, you don't need approval nearly as much. If you choose to confront her about asking too much of you, expecting that you go only to places of her choice, you may find an answer you didn't anticipate. She was assuming everything was fine because you never complained or objected.

Often, when people expect too much of you, you haven't set a boundary. When you do, it becomes much easier to say no and still feel loving.

The better I feel about myself, the easier it is to release old relationships that don't support my growth.

▼▼▼

Often, when you enter recovery, old friends try to pull you back into the kind of life you are struggling to leave. You have been accustomed to abuse so long that these abusive people still feel familiar. It is tricky to be around the kinds of people who still live that life because the pressures for you to conform to your old behavior are very strong. Old relationships carry expectations of the old codependent or addictive you, ready at a moment's notice to run off on a weekend junket that needs your last-minute financial support, or ready to eat at a restaurant that you don't really like and can't really afford. These people do not have your best interests at heart!

As you grow stronger in your recovery and especially as you make new friends who will support your new healthy behavior, your old friends will be less and less attractive to you. It will be easier to let go of the old relationships as you feel better about yourself and your new way of life.

There are always new supportive people to meet, as long as you give yourself the opportunity to be where they are and to make yourself available for friendship.

I now create relationships that nurture me.

▼▼▼

If you usually find yourself in the caretaker or rescuer role, you may relate to the difficulty of being able to sit back and enjoy someone else doing something for you. Jason found this transition an interesting one. He had to find new people in his life who didn't require his constant attention, who liked to give *and* receive instead of just receive.

Jason now notices people who take care of themselves because he knows healthy people have a life-style of caring for themselves. He also watches out for people with compassion who are willing to be strong for another person when the situation calls for it, but who avoid caretaking and enabling. His old girlfriend always wanted him to meet her needs without ever having to say a word. After that experience, Jason especially seeks out people who communicate what they need. His old girlfriend said that he had changed when he wouldn't go out with her anymore. Jason took that as a definite compliment!

Using this affirmation will help keep you focused on looking for different traits in new relationships rather than the kind of response to needy traits that captured you in your old relationships. Listening to what people say about how they take care of themselves, the nurturing they give themselves, is a good indication that if they can be there for themselves, they can be there in a healthy way for others.

If you catch yourself even thinking about rescuing, remember this affirmation and take care of *you* by finding another kind of person to be with.

**I improve what I can offer in my
relationships by taking responsibility
for my abandonment issues.**

▼▼▼

You can unintentionally harm your relationships in many ways if you suffer from fear of abandonment and don't recognize it. In friendship, fear of abandonment can make you unreasonably possessive of a friend's time and jealous of others with whom he or she might also have friendships. In intimate relationships, it can make you want to thoroughly engulf the person that you say you love.

As soon as you face your fear of abandonment, you are in a position to make choices about how to help yourself. Many of us are frightened to be alone because we have never created our own boundaries. When we are in relationships with other people, we "steal" their boundaries, making decisions based on how that other person will react. If we think we are going to lose that person, we feel emotionally naked without a boundary system of our own.

The only healthy antidote to this situation is to become your own person with your own boundaries. Then, if your relationship partner leaves, you are a separate person and don't feel as if your partner is taking all that really matters about you out the door with him or her. Dealing with the infamous "hole in the soul," that deep loneliness in the pit of your stomach that you try to cover up with another person, is definitely hard work, but it is the only way to become a whole person yourself.

When you take responsibility for your fear of abandonment and you gain your own boundaries, you cultivate a real chance of relating to another human being.

I am centered and I am attracted to healthy people in my relationships.

▼▼▼

As you become centered, you will notice that your energy around other people has changed. You feel more confident about yourself, and people in your life will respond to that confidence. Because you feel better about yourself, healthy people will seem more attractive and accessible to you. When you are not in a good place yourself, you rarely feel that you have anything to offer someone who is leading a balanced and healthy life. As your life grows closer and closer to that positive description, you do actually have much more in common with healthy people than with those who have no direction and are in self-destructive patterns.

In your assessment of yourself, if all of you adds up on paper to fairly healthy, give yourself a break and act as if you were healthy until you feel it solidly inside. By the time that happens, you may find that you have done the footwork for a whole new healthy life-style and are ready to leap into it just at the time your feelings about yourself catch up with you.

It is all right to act healthier than you really are because you will attract more health into your life.

I value myself first when considering a relationship.

▼▼▼

When you are lonely and in need of a "fix" from another person, you most likely consider instantly moving in with a new someone to satisfy your ache, completely forgetting about whether the person is a realistic long-range possibility in your life. The first order of business is to give yourself a new set of rules for meeting people and a new set of ways to deal with your impulsivity. The second order of business is to start asking for what you want and need in a relationship, and when you meet someone, think very seriously about whether it will be possible for you to get those wants and needs met with this person.

Before you even think about meeting someone new, think long and hard about valuing yourself today. Then take a look at your past relationships and notice what you usually go for—people who need rescuing, alcoholics, charming con artists, people who never seem to work, self-obsessed beautiful people, artists with no room for you in their lives, workaholics, or deadbeats. Make a mental list of the qualities of these people that attract you and look for them in any potential partner you meet. If you find one, you need to take the time to evaluate. He or she could be potential material for yet another abusive heartbreak.

Valuing yourself first and evaluating the other person before jumping into a relationship is completely opposite to the way you have probably operated in relationships your entire life. You may find it an interesting and nurturing change for you.

When you value *yourself,* you find yourself in much more valuable relationships.

RESPONSIBILITY

▼▼▼

When you bypass the decision to take personal responsibility in a situation and slide back into the victim role by default, your old, helpless childhood feelings will surface. You are placing an outdated belief from your childhood onto a present-day activity. It simply isn't true that there is nothing you can do today, as an adult, to improve a situation. If nothing else, with these affirmations and your increased awareness you can improve your attitude and increase your ability to deal with any situation.

I am responsible for setting only myself straight and keeping only myself on course.

▼▼▼

If you have grown up constantly on guard and aware of your parents' moves so that you could please, duck, or hide just to survive each day, your whole frame of reference becomes focused outside yourself. You react to other people.

For some, this focus on other people developed into rescuing. You felt overly responsible for what happens to other people. You used your energy not in making choices for yourself but in keeping other people "on course." Some women have supported more than one husband through graduate school and startup businesses only to wake up and realize they had not been paying any attention to themselves.

Two 12-Step programs, Co-Dependents Anonymous and Al-Anon, deal excellently with these issues and can help you make the transition from superresponsibility for others to keeping your eyes on yourself. You will be surprised at all you can accomplish when your efforts are directed toward goals for yourself. You will be surprised at how satisfying it will be to have your *own* life.

I am responsible only for my own feelings. I can care about other people, but they control their own feelings.

▼▼▼

One of the traps of an abusive childhood is the "walking on eggshells" syndrome, stifling your behavior and feelings because you might upset the feelings of one or both parents. Even worse, the threat of "Don't do that! You'll upset your father and make him drink (or gamble or run off)," gave you an enormously overblown sense that you had real power over other people's feelings. There was no way for you to know that you were caught in your parents' manipulations, and that it was not at all appropriate for a child to be made responsible for any adult's feelings or behavior.

Today, you are still vulnerable when someone says, "*You* upset me. *You* ruined my afternoon," because of childhood guilt and the old belief that you are responsible for other people's feelings. Working with this affirmation will help you let go of that belief and feel comfortable in the realization that adults are indeed responsible for their own feelings. Circumstances happen to everyone, but as an adult, you can process your feelings and choose your reactions. As you use this affirmation, you will feel much lighter as you release responsibility that others can take on themselves.

I am responsible for creating and leading my own life.

▼▼▼

You were the child of a parent or parents who abused you physically, sexually, or emotionally. Now you are an Adult Child who is affected by that abuse and who chooses to become responsible for creating a new and better life for yourself. Some of you may find it difficult to leave behind the consciousness of being a victim all those years. You feel that if you move on and get healthier, all the evidence of your painful past will disappear, and no one will ever believe what hard times you had! That is understandable, but it is a belief that is keeping you from the kind of life you want to lead. And it means perpetual suffering for you if you don't change this way of thinking.

If you find that you are struggling with this problem, talk to someone. In Adult Children of Alcoholics, Co-Dependents Anonymous, and Incest Survivors Anonymous groups, you will find people who will support you. There are also many qualified therapists with experience in these areas.

Saying or writing this affirmation following the instructions in the Introduction will help you become clear about the right avenue for you. You can create your own pathway to health.

**I ask for what I want as a powerful way
of taking responsibility for myself.**

▼▼▼

You may find, as many Adult Children do, that it is hard for you to ask for what you want. You may still need other people's approval and fear they might find you too aggressive or needy, or—worst-case scenario—they might say no. Remind yourself that while these are all possibilities, none of the feared consequences would be the end of the world. If someone said no, you would survive the experience and probably learn a great deal from it. But there is a good chance that person might say yes.

With your old techniques of whining, cajoling, hinting, and manipulating, you never knew where you stood. You never got a direct answer because you never asked a direct question. Frequently, you were frustrated when someone didn't figure out exactly what it was you wanted.

Leaving the guesswork behind, you should begin to make small requests at first: "Can you give me a hug?" "Will you meet me for the movies on Saturday afternoon?" That way, your risks are small, but you *are* taking responsibility for yourself. Increase the size of your requests gradually. Honor your right to ask, and respect the right of others to decline. Using this affirmation before you make any request will help you feel more confident as you develop an entirely different way of being responsible for yourself.

I am responsible for everything I choose to give to others and for everything I allow myself to receive.

▼▼▼

How often have you heard the following: "I had to give my boss an expensive gift. How would it look if I gave her something small?" As an Adult Child, you may not value yourself in any of your relationships, so you choose to buy your way in with gifts that are more expensive than what is often appropriate for the occasion or for your finances. When you give of yourself way beyond your limitations, you sell yourself short. But you blame it on external circumstances instead of seeing that you feel you aren't enough. Allowing others to give inappropriately to you can also make you feel uncomfortable, but you are responsible for setting your boundaries to maintain your own comfort zone. Begin to monitor your giving and receiving. How many times do you pick up the check for lunch or give birthday gifts when you don't receive them? Take responsibility for your choices in light of your feelings about yourself. You can make changes when you come out of denial.

Giving and receiving can be a way to get closer to others when we are honest with ourselves and responsible for what we are doing.

I am responsible for my own recovery.

▼▼▼

Although you may have been guided to a program, a counselor, or group therapy, your follow-through with any of these recovery processes has been entirely up to you. Only you can make the commitment to yourself that you want to process your childhood pain in order to live a healthier and happier life today.

This doesn't mean that you have to do it all alone. Going to support groups and finding friends that you can talk to while you are going through the healing process is a responsible and sensible way to make the process safer and more comfortable. Getting the right kind of support demonstrates intelligence and independence because it gives a broader base to your recovery.

Even with this support in place, it is still up to you to reach out to others, to keep in contact with your new friends and call them when you need to talk during a rough period. Your willingness is completely your responsibility. You can remind yourself with this affirmation that the buck does indeed stop here, that your recovery is *your* responsibility.

I am responsible for providing for myself financially.

▼▼▼

Too many Adult Children take out their anger at their abusive parents by refusing to become responsible for themselves financially, as if that would ease their pain and make up for past deprivation. It isn't a solution. If you find that you have persistent financial difficulties, you need to find help to identify your specific problems and then deal with them. Debtors Anonymous can certainly help you with this, and there are also competent financial and credit counselors in every city.

It may surprise you to know that this difficulty has very little to do with the amount of money that you make to support yourself. There are Adult Children with six-figure salaries who are still not responsible in the area of personal finance, because they believe that somehow they either can't or shouldn't have to be responsible for their finances. Perhaps their parents retained control by telling them they could never manage their money, or their resentment at never being properly cared for as children came out as an unrealized expectation today.

No matter what might have happened in your abusive childhood to cause this, having an attitude today of responsibility for yourself financially is the key to helping you recover, along with the belief that you are completely *able* to be responsible no matter what.

SELF-ESTEEM

▼▼▼

What is self-esteem and how do you get it? Everyone who has low or no self-esteem asks this question at one time or another. People with self-esteem have a positive attitude and know they are of value to themselves and to others with whom they have relationships. People with self-esteem feel comfortable inside their own skin, respect the boundaries of others and have no need to violate them, and do not demand instant gratification or perfection. People with self-esteem have an air of general well-being and look forward to the adventure of each day, one day at a time.

How you develop self-esteem is up to you. In some cases, you need to make drastic changes in order to start the process. To make those decisions, you need to take an inventory of your life as it is today, looking honestly at the healthy and unhealthy people and activities you associate with. Then you can choose to remove from your life those people and activities that are harmful to your growth as a person.

As you go through this process in every area of your life, from the beliefs you hold to the foods you eat, you will find that as you clean up your act, your feelings about yourself will improve greatly. This is the beginning of improving your self-esteem. The following affirmations can help you along your way.

I feel good about myself.

▼▼▼

This affirmation gets right to the heart of the matter of self-esteem. When you use it, it pulls you back into knowing exactly what really matters in the whole scheme of things: feeling good about yourself. If you are alone in the house or in your car, say this affirmation out loud slowly and with feeling 10 times. See if you don't start to relax and even begin to smile after the first several minutes.

This affirmation is about you, right now, and despite anything that can happen to you, you can go right on deciding to feel good about yourself.

My actions support my feeling good about myself.

▼▼▼

When you act in a way that supports your self-esteem, you strengthen the inner sense of yourself that has received negative treatment for so long in your life. When you feel good about the new ways in which you are interacting with people, your confidence that you really *can* be effective is bolstered just a little bit more.

It is difficult to feel good about yourself when you don't act on your own behalf. Leaving behind self-destructive behaviors such as addictions and codependency gives you the room to start creating new, positive behaviors. Staying aware of your behaviors and making corrections on a daily basis when they are necessary are part of a healthy recovery program. There are times when acting "as if" you were confident works so well that the action is carried out beautifully, and the next thing you know, you really can do what you didn't know you could do.

When you have a program of positive actions and you consciously practice thinking well about yourself, your self-esteem will definitely be on the rise.

I can let others be disappointed in me and still feel good about myself.

▼▼▼

One hallmark of low self-esteem is the desperate need for approval. If you don't feel at all good about yourself, it becomes a matter of survival to have others approve of you. This terrible fear of letting other people down is part of what drives people to drink, overeat, gamble, and be promiscuous.

In recovery, you gain self-esteem little by little, using affirmations, writing in your journal, and spending time with people who make you feel good. You will gradually come to depend less and less on pleasing others in order to feel centered and OK.

One day you will surprise yourself and say, "No, I don't think I'll go with you to the movies. I need to take care of some things at home this evening." What your friend thinks won't even be an issue any longer because you are doing what is best for you.

A lifetime load is lifted off. Your life is really becoming your own now, and you can look in the mirror and say to yourself, "I *am* recovering!"

Self-esteem expands your freedom.

I enjoy hearing sincere compliments from others.

▼▼▼

As your self-esteem increases, you begin to feel better and better about receiving compliments from others because your insides now match the good outside things that you are hearing about yourself. Previously, if you were dressed up to go out for dinner and someone told you that you looked wonderful, you felt shame rather than joy because there was nothing inside you that could resonate with the compliment. In fact, when someone said something nice to you, you actually ended up feeling worse about yourself than you did if you were criticized. Now *that* felt real!

You have come a long way from those childhood days, and your feelings about yourself are entirely different. You now get honest feedback from your new friends, and you have created a different image of yourself by interacting with people who are supportive of your growth and tell you so consistently. When you feel good about yourself, the world can become a nurturing place filled with people who tell you nice, honest things about you.

It's amazing what a change your inside world can do to your outside world!

I am attracted to people who help me feel good about myself.

▼▼▼

If you want your self-esteem to grow stronger, it is very helpful to be around people who in turn help you feel good about yourself. When you get a raise at work, it's good to be with someone who congratulates you and allows you to see all the good that you have accomplished by doing your job well and by staying there and getting a raise. It is much easier to enjoy your success with someone else supporting you.

On the other hand, it doesn't help your efforts to develop self-esteem if you get a raise and someone says, "Gee, only $20 a week. That hardly makes a difference," or "I knew several other people in the firm who got raises much more quickly. What do you suppose held yours up?" Instead of being supported, you find yourself defending something for which a real friend would be congratulating you.

If you detect that you continue to be around people who are not your real friends, it may be time to put some distance between you and them and not share the good things that are happening in your life with these belittling buddies. Making these choices is difficult but necessary.

Honor your own intuition and feelings. Pay attention to how your body feels around people. If it feels relaxed and strong and you feel comfortable, most likely you are with people who are healthy for you. If you feel nervous or put down, it is time to reassess and make positive choices for yourself.

Surrounding yourself with people who make you feel good and who support you is one effective way to build your self-esteem.

**I value my own journey through life
and realize I am responsible for
keeping myself on my own path.**

▼▼▼

Only when you value yourself and your own life can you stay centered and pursue your own goals. There are a lot of people who would like to use you to further their goals in life, and they will do it if you let them. This can happen in personal relationships, in business, and in volunteer organizations. If you are unwilling to commit to yourself first, someone else will get you to commit to them.

Yvonne had worked hard to create her own life after her divorce. She had become active in Co-Dependents Anonymous and in a local environmental organization, where she was involved in running the office and raising money. She had been dating Steve off and on for several years, and when he moved to another state they still remained friends. One day she got a call from Steve; he was in town and wanted to see her.

They met for coffee and he "announced" that he would like to initiate a serious relationship with her, that he wanted to start up a new business where he was living, and that he wanted to share his life with someone. Yvonne could see the old trap: giving up her life to help a man get his own life going. She thanked Steve for the compliment but told him that she had changed.

Even though Steve objected and acted wounded, Yvonne was able to stand her ground and say straightforwardly, "This is how I feel, and there really isn't anything to discuss. I would like to stay friends, but that is all I have to offer you."

Value your own life. It is the only one you have.

Now that I experience self-esteem, I no longer attract abuse.

▼▼▼

When you truly feel good about yourself on an unconscious level, others intuitively feel it. A person who is accustomed to taking advantage of or abusing others will simply stay away from someone who sends out signals that say, "I matter to myself and I can take care of myself." Like a burglar who sees an alarm signal on a house, such a person will move on to easier prey.

The best way to prevent being a victim is to feel good about yourself—a tall order, since victims generally have very poor self-esteem, especially after an incident. If you are aware, however, you can consciously turn the energy of a victimizing incident around, work hard on feeling good about yourself in spite of the abuse that you have suffered, and give yourself the chance for a future without further abuse.

You matter, no matter what has happened to you.

SPIRITUAL GROWTH

▼▼▼

In all programs of recovery, as you recover physically, mentally, and emotionally, your awareness will keep expanding and your perspective will keep broadening. When you reach this stage of integration, you may find your spirituality naturally evolving. You will feel a stronger connection to other people and a consciousness of a Higher Self within you, a part of you that you can reach through meditation, prayer, or simply being still and relaxed.

Some programs of recovery, such as the 12-Step programs, revolve around reliance on a "power greater than yourself, a god of your understanding." Recognizing the existence of this Higher Power is the backbone of these programs, but the emphasis is strictly spiritual and not religious in any sense.

To develop your spirituality, you need to place your focus on three different areas: the area of being still or meditating, the area of living in the present moment, and the area of developing your ability to love. The following affirmations will help you work in these areas.

**I have faith that there is a power
greater than myself giving me guidance.**

▼▼▼

If you have faith in a power greater than yourself, it may
lie in a frame of reference beyond what we as human beings
know. Faith gives you a sense of perspective about your place
on this planet and can do much to reduce the grandiosity
that overcomes people when they are trying to run away from
themselves and their pain.

The support that can come into your life when you trust
that Higher Power is working for your greater good and is
beyond measure. When you are able to turn your life over
to the care of that power, whether it is your Higher Self or
a god of your understanding, the burden of feeling that you
have to know everything is lifted. Living becomes easier.

Trusting in a power greater than yourself can help you see
everything about your life in perspective.

I meditate every day to be still and get in touch with the core of my being.

▼▼▼

There are many kinds of meditations, including chanting, invoking a mantra, walking, and breath counting. If you want to learn to meditate, the book *How to Meditate* by Lawrence LeShan will give you a good introduction. Or you can ask at your local spiritual bookshop for the names of local groups that teach meditation.

If you want to get into a quiet state without using a formal method, sit down in a spot near the ocean or sit at the base of a large tree and close your eyes. Think of the peace of nature around you and let go of whatever you are attached to right at that moment. See if you can feel the connection between you and all that is around you in nature, the connection between the core of your being and the energy of the world.

The importance of being still, of feeling the center of yourself and the presence of a spiritual power, lies in strengthening the connection to that spiritual core of your being, the part of you that has survived all the abuse and still remains strong. When you are in touch with your own spiritual center and how you connect to a Higher Power and to everyone around you, you begin to feel the peace that you have heard other people experience. You deserve to feel this serenity, so give yourself the gift of meditation.

You connect with your own strength when you meditate.

My new connectedness to other people contributes to my spiritual growth.

▼▼▼

When you were alone with your pain, and you thought you were the only one who suffered this way, you probably never imagined you could feel the connectedness you are feeling now after being in recovery. Most of us feel so much stronger when we are able to connect to a power greater than ourselves as well as to other people.

After Tanya joined a 12-Step program, she felt that her connection to her Higher Power deepened the closeness she felt to other people. She felt surrounded by the loving force of something much greater than herself, and she surrendered her sense of isolation. She met a woman from her hometown, and they started to spend time together, a welcome change from her previously solitary activities.

Our spiritual connection can strengthen our connection to other people.

I maintain a spiritual plan in all areas of my life.

▼▼▼

Spirituality isn't confined to the time we spend in meditation or in meetings to enhance our connection to our Higher Power. We can make a plan to practice our spiritual principles in the outside world. This is the final step in all the 12-Step programs, and it works very well for those who want to live a life guided by a power greater than themselves.

Before beginning his personal recovery, Ed had a difficult time in all his working situations because he held grudges against people who he felt were causing him difficulty. When he came to understand the principle of forgiveness and how it helped him deal with his feelings about other people, he started becoming less disgruntled with those working beside him and more content with himself.

Using a spiritual plan in all areas of your life can simplify your relationships at work and in your personal life.

My pain has contributed to my spiritual growth.

▼▼▼

Being grateful for your pain is not easy, but for some people, pain has been the touchstone for their spiritual growth. Pain is certainly a call to wake up and change, or there will very likely be more pain. It can often guide you into a program of spirituality that transforms your life.

When Danielle left her husband because she was no longer willing to put up with his drinking, she suddenly had to create resources for herself in order to survive. She went back to work as a bank teller because she had had a good job record at her local branch bank before she had become pregnant. She also turned to Al-Anon for help with her alcoholic husband. What Danielle discovered was a network of women who could love her through her painful time and could teach her what it means to work a spiritual program. While things are very hard for Danielle as a single mother, she now has the support she needs to help her use her pain to cultivate spiritual growth.

Out of your pain, you can often find your way to spiritual growth.

TAKING CARE OF YOURSELF

▼▼▼

Because you grew up with abusive parents who used you to meet their own needs rather than caring for you and nurturing you, you learned how to meet other people's needs in such a way that it felt like you were absolutely taking care of yourself. As long as you made others happy, you felt happy. It was a subtle and compelling trap. Overcoming the pattern of meeting other people's needs means that you have to make changes in the way you respond.

Now you can allow yourself time to think, to say, "We'll see," or "I'll get back to you," or even to change your mind if you impulsively said yes. Part of taking care of yourself is thinking clearly about what consequences meeting someone else's needs can make in your life. You must also make sure that you care for yourself physically by eating nourishing foods and exercising regularly. Putting your health and well-being first above other people, places, and things means that you *are* taking care of yourself.

I only say yes to those requests that allow me to maintain my health.

▼▼▼

So many times you will be tempted to respond to a request with an immediate yes, because things were described as being a great deal simpler than they actually turn out to be. Say, for instance, a friend asks, "Can you drive me to work for a few days? My car is in the garage." It sounds like a reasonable request, and you answer, "Yes, I can do that." But as it turns out, your friend is never on time. You wait more than half an hour at the end of each day, sacrificing your exercise or afternoon rest time that keeps you mentally and physically healthy.

At this time in your life, your health and well-being are your most important considerations. You need to talk with your friend and tell him that you agreed to give him a ride, not an extra hour of waiting time.

You used to feel that if you gave your word, you could not go back on it even if the others involved did not keep their word. This was abuse, though more subtle than you may have been used to.

Today, it is all right to give yourself permission to take care of yourself in any situation, and to give yourself first priority.

I get enough rest to feel refreshed
mentally and physically.

▼▼▼

Very often you might have played the role of the adult in your house, feeling you had to take on the tasks of cooking, doing the laundry, or caring for other children when your mother and father weren't able to do so. And you kept going to school, doing the best you possibly could, handling more responsibility than many adults.

Frequently, you didn't get enough sleep. The fights kept you awake, and there was always too much to do to take care of yourself and the other children. You got used to deprivation in many areas, but definitely in the areas of rest and recreation. Today, you can make choices on your own behalf. Keep this affirmation in mind every day, and when you start to rescue people or situations because you feel that *someone* has to be responsible, slow down and think about what you are asking of yourself.

Take the time for rest and play.

I choose recreational activities that make me happy physically and mentally.

▼▼▼

Getting in touch with what you really like to do may take some experimentation. If you have been used to ignoring your own likes in favor of pleasing someone else, or your wishes were ignored as a child because they conflicted with what your parents wanted you to do, you may need to go through an uncovering, discovering, and discarding process before you find things to do that give you real pleasure and satisfaction. Whether it's playing volleyball, lifting weights, or writing poetry, it is your turn to do what you like.

In many 12-Step recovery groups, people in recovery are doing things they never dared do before—oil painting, dancing, even fencing—and their feelings about themselves are changing.

When you truly enjoy yourself, the good feelings carry over into all other areas of your life.

I am loving and kind to myself in all situations.

▼▼▼

Beating up on yourself on a regular basis may be an old habit that you will choose to change. If all you heard from your parents as a child was criticism, the "committee" in your head will continue to repeat those critical voices, and they will still give you their negative opinions long after you have left home. If you can catch yourself when you let that committee take over after you have made a mistake, stop them with a strong statement such as, "I don't need you anymore." Talk to yourself affectionately, even hug yourself, and you will be on the path to loving yourself in all situations.

You can also use this affirmation to give you support in doing thoughtful things for yourself, such as buying tickets to a sporting event, a concert, or the theater, eating out at a special restaurant, or taking a drive in the moonlight.

Practice doing the things for yourself that you would do for someone you love.

I give myself permission to renegotiate any agreement I make.

▼▼▼

The sadness of feeling betrayed over and over by broken promises when you were a child made you swear you would never break a promise or a commitment, no matter what! At the same time, because you have been attracted to people that evoke in you the same feelings that you experienced with your unreliable family, you are frequently entering into agreements with untrustworthy people.

However, you do have a way of taking care of yourself through the "I've thought it over and I've changed my mind" statement. Giving yourself permission to renegotiate, to change your mind, is the way "normal" people operate in the world. Situations change. Your feelings can legitimately change. You can give yourself permission to jump off a ship that is going to take you down.

If you are in a good job and you want to stay there, but you feel you are worth more money, you have the right to ask for a raise. By using this affirmation to give you support, you can feel strong enough to renegotiate agreements you have made in any area of your life.

Negotiating for yourself protects you for yourself.

Today I use my energy on my own behalf.

▼▼▼

By constructively protecting yourself from abusive people, it is not necessary for you to spend all your energy on self-defense or on somehow escaping from your current situation into fantasy just to get through the day.

In the past, when you had no boundaries, your energy was available for others to "rip off." Sometimes, you did their work for them. At other times, you were the emotional garbage pail in which they dumped the trash of their most recent failure. After being injured by one of these abusive people, you obsessed for days over how it happened and how you could somehow rectify the situation, draining yourself of the energy you needed to move forward in your own life. This obsession was equally destructive for you.

Now that you have boundaries, it is possible for you to choose not to be the recipient of someone else's energy drain. By detaching and containing your emotions so that they aren't available to another person for exploitation, you will quickly find a great deal more of your energy available for yourself.

I can leave a situation that becomes abusive to me.

▼▼▼

One of the tough things about being a child with abusive parents is that, effectively, you can't leave. Adult Children did run away when they were young but often ended up in the hands of juvenile authorities, which was not a solution to the pain. They simply got on the merry-go-round of Juvenile Hall or foster care, or were sent back home. As a child, you learned to endure unbearable pain and to witness unspeakable behavior, which you never need to do again. But you have to make yourself aware of the situations you are experiencing and what options are open to you.

Having endured so much abuse, one of the difficulties you may experience is that you don't feel abuse when it is happening. You are numb. Joining a therapy group or 12-Step program is helpful. Listening to other people's stories can give you a basis for evaluating your own situations. Also, you can talk to others who have been through similar experiences and ask what they would do in a given situation of yours.

Knowing that you have choices today and that you are not trapped the way you were as a child can give you the ability to appropriately sort your situation out. You can learn to recognize your pain and free yourself from it.

TRUST

▼▼▼

If you were to try to guess how "normal" people deal with trust issues, you would probably be surprised at how cautious they are and how much sizing up and looking out for themselves they do before making a decision about a person, place, or thing. Because denial was so common in your family, you learned to discount your own perceptions, feelings, and thoughts.

Today, continuing that pattern places you at the mercy of outside influences when you make decisions. It particularly makes you a prime target for con men, because you automatically dismiss all your doubts about such people just as you had to dismiss all your feelings to survive in your family.

When you are around people who don't give out signals that cause you to have doubts, you don't feel comfortable. There is nothing to suppress. They seem too straightforward and honest, so you generally pull away from the very people who could become good friends. Allowing yourself to become aware of your real reactions to people and situations and trusting those reactions can make your life much safer. When you find yourself zoning out around a person or in a situation, take note of it and try to see what information you are trying to suppress. The following affirmations can help increase your level of trust in yourself and others.

I am learning to trust people who are worthy of trust.

▼▼▼

Joel had never told anyone he loved them since the day his father instructed him to fall backward off the porch, promising to catch him. His father let Joel fall to the ground as a lesson that he could not trust anyone, not even his own father. Joel was nearing 50, had never married, and was disheartened that he was so afraid to express his love, even though he felt he was loving.

Slowly, by facing his trust issues, Joel realized that his father had made a mistake and that he had been punishing the whole world for it by not trusting anyone. He let go of his anger and carefully started to trust in situations where he felt safe. Today, Joel is happily married to a woman with two teenage children. He allows himself to take risks within the family and tells each of them every day how much he loves them and how fortunate he feels to have found a family.

When your parents teach you not to trust, that lack of trust can affect your whole life. You may not make good judgments about who is trustworthy and who is not. You may keep trusting the wrong people because they feel comfortable on a subconscious level. Later, you will wake up and realize you have repeated the pattern one more time. Now you can recognize those mesmerizing feelings when they happen to you. When you are about to trust someone without knowing who they are, step back and give yourself time to assess. Talk to a friend before you make any decisions.

The nature of trust is slow and gentle.

I trust my own inner knowing.

▼▼▼

For all these years, you have learned to deny, minimize, and repress your feelings. You also learned to discount any voice inside you that cried out against the abuse you were suffering. Your feelings and that inner voice will guide you toward health today. The voice that warned you about dangers as a child is still inside you, waiting for you to listen and become free to trust your own inner knowing. Only when you can trust yourself can you be less vulnerable to falling into old patterns with people who are destructive, or into old situations that will benefit others at a high cost to you.

If you can spend time quietly in a naturally beautiful place, the chances of getting in touch with your inner knowing are enhanced. After you are well in tune with yourself, when you take time to be still to get in touch with your inner knowing, the distractions of being at home or at work won't interfere. Meditation is a good way to make your inner contact.

If you practice contacting your inner self, you can call on its wisdom whenever you need it.

I trust my judgment about who I can confide in and what is appropriate to confide.

▼▼▼

Since it was against the rules for you to talk about what was going on in your house when you were growing up, you may have had no idea who was a safe person or what was a safe place to tell your secrets. Pouring your heart out to someone has therapeutic value, but you need to be willing to confront and process the feelings that come up, or you will find yourself needing to vent everything again and again. Continuously dumping everything on someone else doesn't give you any permanent release or growth. You may also offend people who have not given you permission to use them as emotional garbage pails, thus alienating current friends and potential friends by not respecting their boundaries.

Your choice of who to talk to is highly individual, and you are the right person to make such a choice for yourself. You can talk with a professional therapist, priest, rabbi, or minister, or attend a private support group or a 12-Step program. It is very important for you to feel comfortable working through your childhood abuse, and you can trust your intuition to help you choose the safest people for you to confide in.

You need to make decisions about confiding in people and to trust yourself to make those decisions for your benefit.

I trust my Higher Power to help me heal the pain of my childhood.

▼▼▼

Having trust in your Higher Power to help you work through all the pain you suffered as a child gives you an ally in the most difficult times of your recovery. However, you might also ask, "Where was that Higher Power when all these things happened to me?" You may even go through a stage of being angry at your Higher Power for allowing the abuse to happen.

Persisting in blaming others, even your Higher Power, does not help with healing. Accepting what has happened to you and looking for all the comfort and healing that are being offered to you is the most effective way to get on with your life.

In their third step, the 12-Step programs suggest "turning our will and our lives over to God as we understand him." Having the ability to trust in your own Higher Power means you can let go of a lot of the burdens in your life that you have carried ever since you can remember. Developing your spirituality by trusting in your own Higher Power can also open your heart to the love that others want to give you.

Visualize giving your pain to your Higher Power and taking in all the healing love that is being offered to you.

I trust myself in the face of questioning from others.

▼▼▼

When you start to change in recovery, you become less dependent and begin to trust yourself and your feelings. Your family or friends may start asking, "Just what exactly is going on with you? A few months ago, you weren't Miss Independent and things were working OK. Now you seem to know everything and you don't need us anymore."

There is an issue here you need to address: all those people in your life may feel threatened and have an investment in keeping you as you were. Unfortunately, your friends and spouses may have a difficult time adjusting to your new confidence and lack of dependence. You are choosing what is happening in your own life for the first time, and the change will take time to get used to.

Frequently, if you trust yourself and stay patient and calm, the others in your life will come around. Giving yourself the trust that you have always given to others causes the equilibrium in all of your relationships to shift. It may cause everyone discomfort initially, but in the long run, if you are much happier with yourself, the people that stay in relationships with you will be much happier too.

If you trust yourself while making changes that others question, in time those others will come to trust you also.

YOUR BODY

▼▼▼

Learning how to care for your body is an important part of your recovery from the abuse you suffered. As a child, your body was often the instrument for physical and sexual abuse, and you became ashamed and often dissociated from any feelings your body might have, just in order to survive. Now you are waking up. You can discard the numbness that covered you like a security blanket through dangerous times as you become more secure and develop new ways of dealing with the world. This is, after all, your only body for the journey through this life.

Placing value on your body rather than using every ounce of its energy and burning out will be new to you. It takes getting used to. But you need to respect your body if it is going to carry you the full distance in your life without serious problems. These affirmations will help you get in touch with what your body needs to be healthy.

**I take good care of my body and treat
it lovingly and with respect.**

▼▼▼

When you suffered physical and sexual abuse, you knew how to detach from your body and from the pain in order to stay alive. No one can carry that much hurt as a child and stay functional. To focus on your body would have meant focusing on the pain, so you frequently ignored anything that went on with your body. It's hard to forget old ways of relating to yourself and to start letting your body feel again.

Beginning a program of sensory recovery is essential in learning to touch your whole world—the objects around you, animals, children, other adults, and yourself. Once your body can feel again, it becomes easier for you to give it the proper care, nutrition, and exercise. Now that you are awakening and letting your body feel, your body really belongs to you for the first time.

I follow my exercise and health
routines faithfully.

▼▼▼

Learning to exercise on a regular basis will help you stay centered as you work on integrating the pain of your childhood. It is a proven antidote to depression and encourages balance when you keep up a good routine. Most likely, no one in your family exercised on a regular basis because your lives were disrupted by the drama of arguments and frequently by substance abuse, which brought on child abuse.

Exercising regularly, even if it is a half-hour walk in your neighborhood three times a week, will usher in more positive and healthier feelings about yourself.

I listen to my body's messages and act on the signals it sends me for my well-being.

▼▼▼

When you were a child and your stomach was tied in knots when your mother or father came near, you couldn't run away. You were too small, and you had to stay put and take whatever happened to you. Eventually, your stomach learned to ignore the signals sent by your fear, and you became numb in order to endure the abuse. It is hard to relax after all those years and allow your stomach to once again send you messages of danger. You need to learn to honor your body.

When someone potentially unhealthy to your well-being comes near you and your body tells you something is dangerous, you need to listen and take more time to assess the situation.

Use your intelligence and your body to make the best decisions for your well-being.

I eat healthy foods that strengthen
my body.

▼▼▼

One of the most important components of a successful recovery is making sure that you have the physical strength to do it! You need endurance and energy to "grow up again" because the stresses of going through "adolescence" again as an adult and grieving the losses of your childhood will deplete you physically if you do not give your body support during the process. In the past, you may have paid little attention to what you ate, choosing fast foods like hamburgers and fried chicken out of lifelong habit.

Today it is much easier to eat well. Even fast-food chains offer fresh salads, and corner convenience stores have packages of fresh-cut and peeled vegetables. You can carry a piece of fruit to eat for your afternoon snack instead of potato chips or candy. Making small choices for better nutrition adds up at the end of the week.

If nutrition is a new area for you, visit your local health-food store and ask about basic books on the subject. You may want to request the names of some recommended nutritionists in your area who could help you learn about food values and combinations as well as vitamin supplements.

If you have used food only as fuel to keep going, or have abused food to try to ease your pain, eating well is the start of a wonderful new adventure.

I take time each day to relax my body and my mind.

▼▼▼

One way that you can give yourself comfort is to develop beneficial behaviors that you do for yourself routinely each day. Taking five minutes to stretch each morning after getting up is good for your body and mind. If you were the recipient of much violence in your childhood and are suffering stiffness and pain as you grow older, yoga or stretching exercises can reduce the pain and greatly enhance your mobility. Taking walks at least three times a week is not only relaxing but wonderful for your physical health. Soaking in a hot bath filled with Epsom or other mineral salts seems to pull the soreness out of tense and tired muscles. Sitting quietly or meditating for 10 to 20 minutes each day can calm and center you and also provide a time to gain clarity on what is going on in your life.

The most important thing is to choose something you like to do, something that you will be willing to make time for consistently every day of your life.

I give my body permission to feel
whatever is really going on.

▼▼▼

After all the years of abuse, it is possible that you had to shut down almost totally and be unable to feel, just to survive the reality you were living in. As a child, you weren't allowed to cry or complain when you felt pain. If you did, you would be punished or humiliated, so you endured it, ignored the signals your body sent you, and dissociated from your body—anything to get through the horrible moments. Now, as an adult, you may be injured and not seek treatment because you simply don't feel pain in proportion to the reality of your injuries or illnesses.

Teresa's physical therapist told her that she had the highest tolerance for pain he had ever observed. She was quite proud of that until she realized its implications for her health. It is important to learn to feel again so that you can experience real physical pleasure and will not automatically deny your pain when you are sick or injured. To wake up physically takes patience and willingness to spend time giving your Inner Child lots of sensory experiences: massages, quiet time in a jacuzzi, or barefoot walks on the beach, a grassy lawn, or a field, just to have contact with the earth.

Acknowledging what your body is really experiencing, validating it with another person until you can trust your own receptivity, is the beginning of encouraging the integration of your body and your mind as a whole.

My body is special, and I treasure it.

▼▼▼

Being respectful of your body, taking time to learn how to meet its needs, helps you to become healthy and to maintain that health. This affirmation may bring up that old "committee" of voices that may say things like, "Your body is ugly. Who do you think you are kidding?" Remember to acknowledge the committee with a gentle "Thank you for sharing" and continue saying the affirmation.

You need all the support you can give yourself to transform your old attitude of discounting your body into the new attitude of thinking that it is something special. The specialness does not have anything to do with the way you look; it has to do with realizing that whatever is an integral part of you, like your body, will always be special to *you* if not to anyone else. Choosing to love and treasure your body takes away amazing amounts of stress from your life. Taking time each day to care for your body lets you experience love coming into you no matter what else has gone on during your day.

Remember that your body *is* special and needs nurturing every day.

I enjoy good health and well-being.

▼▼▼

Part of recovery is gaining a solid sense of good health and well-being in spite of whatever physical limitations you might have. This may be the first time it ever occurred to you that you could actually feel a great deal better. The years of abuse may have affected your muscles and bones, from which you still experience pain. And enduring the abuse may have so stressed your immune system that you will need to consciously build yourself up.

What may seem like miraculous leaps into wellness are definitely possible with faith, hope, and hard work. See how it feels to stand in front of the mirror and say, "I enjoy good health and well-being." If you have suffered for some time with a chronic condition, you may encounter resistance from your body and your mind. Acknowledge it and keep right on saying the affirmation out loud, solidly, so that you can feel it resonate in your chest. Become very aware of any negative thoughts you have during the day and let them go as often as you can—particularly anger, which seems to aggravate pain and depress the immune system. If possible, consult a health professional for guidance.

By consciously changing your negative thoughts and pursuing the improvement of your physical condition, you can help your whole body become much healthier, and you can experience the exhilarating feeling of well-being, whatever your limitations.

I am comfortable in keeping my body relaxed and healthy.

▼▼▼

At first it feels foreign to you, letting go of all the tension you normally carry in your body as a matter of course. You've been on "red alert" your whole life, never knowing what was going to happen next. Now you have given yourself permission to relax, consciously relax, because you have chosen a quieter, calmer environment in which to live today. After a few months of practice, it really does feel comfortable and not against the rules to take such good care of yourself.

Working with all the affirmations about your body lifts you to a level of health that you never envisioned possible. Instead of causing you incessant fatigue, exercising regularly makes your body feel much stronger and more ready to work and enjoy your daily life. You are actually comfortable feeling this healthy and having that "caffeine edge" gone. What a change!

You are quieter and calmer. Your body feels much better. You are ready to enjoy life at its best.

ABOUT THE AUTHORS

▼▼▼

Steven Farmer, M.A., M.F.C.C., is Founder and Director of the Center for Adult Children of Abusive Parents and maintains a private counseling practice specializing in integrative healing work with adult children. He has been a featured speaker for a number of national conferences and programs and has appeared on many national television and radio programs.

Juliette Anthony, M.A., M.S., is an independent research consultant, indexer, and writer. She assists other writers and helps non-profit organizations with grant proposals. She has been active in the recovery movement for ten years and lives in Los Angeles.